OZ CLARKE'S
WINE COMPANION

BURGUNDY

GUIDE
CLIVE COATES MW

De Agostini *Editions*

HOW TO USE THIS BOOK

MAPS
For further information on the wine regions see the Fold-out Map.

Each tour in the book has a map to accompany it. These are not detailed road maps; readers are advised to buy such maps to avoid local navigation difficulties.

═══ Motorway (*Autoroute*)

▬▬▬ Major road

──── Minor road

┈┈┈┈ Other road

FACT FILES
Each tour has an accompanying fact file, which lists sources of information on the region, markets and festivals, and where to buy wine. There is also a short listing of hotels and restaurants.

(H) Hotel
(R) Restaurant

To give an indication of prices, we have used a simple rating system.

(F)   Inexpensive
(F)(F)   Moderate
(F)(F)(F) Expensive

WINE PRODUCERS
Producers' names in small capitals refer to entries in the A–Z on page 72.

Visiting arrangements
✓ Visitors welcome
⊘ By appointment
✗ No visitors

Wine styles made
● Red
◐ White
◑ Rosé

Please note that guidebook information is inevitably subject to change. We suggest that, wherever possible, you telephone in advance to check addresses, opening times, etc.

While every care has been taken in preparing this guide, the publishers cannot accept any liability for any consequence arising from the use of information contained in it.

First published by De Agostini Editions Griffin House 161 Hammersmith Road London W6 8SD

Distributed in the U.S. by Stewart, Tabori & Chang, a division of US Media Holdings Inc 115 West 18th Street, 5th Floor New York NY 10011

Distributed in Canada by General Publishing Company Ltd 30 Lesmill Road, Don Mills Ontario M3B 2T6

Oz Clarke's Wine Companion: Burgundy copyright © 1997 Websters International Publishers

Fold-out Map copyright © 1997 Websters International Publishers Text copyright © 1997 Oz Clarke Maps copyright © 1997 Websters International Publishers Some maps and text have been adapted from *Oz Clarke's Wine Atlas* copyright © 1995 Websters International Publishers

Guide copyright © 1997 Websters International Publishers

Created and designed by Websters International Publishers Ltd Axe & Bottle Court 70 Newcomen Street London SE1 1YT

UK ISBN: 1 86212 033 1 A CIP catalogue record for this book is available from the British Library.

US ISBN: 1 86212 037 4 Library of Congress Catalog Card Number 97–065429

OZ CLARKE
Oz Clarke is one of the world's leading wine experts, with a formidable reputation based on his extensive wine knowledge and accessible, no-nonsense approach. He appears regularly on BBC Television and has won all the major wine-writing awards in the USA and UK. His bestselling titles include *Oz Clarke's Wine Atlas*, *Oz Clarke's Pocket Wine Guide* and the *Microsoft Wine Guide* CD-ROM.

CLIVE COATES MW
Master of Wine, Clive Coates writes for most of the world's serious wine magazines and lectures in Europe and the USA. His fine wine magazine, *The Vine*, is circulated throughout the world. His books include *Grands Vins*, the *Finest Châteaux of Bordeaux* and *Côte d'Or, a Celebration of the Great Wines of Burgundy*.

Associate Editorial Director Fiona Holman
Associate Art Director Nigel O'Gorman
Editor Pauline Savage
Art Editor Christopher Howson
Sub-editor Gwen Rigby
Editorial Assistant Emma Richards
Wine Consultant Phillip Williamson
DTP Jonathan Harley
Index Naomi Good
Editorial Director Claire Harcup
Pictorial Cartography Keith and Sue Gage, Contour Designs
Pictorial Map Editor Wink Lorch
Touring Maps European Map Graphics

Colour separations by Columbia Offset, Singapore
Printed in Hong Kong

Photographs:
Front cover Pernand-Vergelesses is best known for its white Corton-Charlemagne Grand Cru.
Page 1 The small village of Auxey-Duresses is in a side valley away from the main Côte de Beaune slope.
Page 3 Pinot Noir is Burgundy's great red grape variety.

Contents

Introduction

Burgundy is not just one wine region of closely meshed villages all making similar wines – it is the umbrella term for the vineyards that start at Chablis, only a couple of hours' drive from Paris, and stretch way down south to Beaujolais, almost to the gates of Lyon. In between Chablis' mineral-scented, bone-dry whites and the juicy, glugging reds of Beaujolais are the Côte d'Or (divided into Côte de Nuits and Côte de Beaune), the source of just about all Burgundy's most stupendous reds and whites; the Côte Chalonnaise with its pleasant, but sometimes rather unconfident reds and whites; and the Mâconnais, which produces potentially excellent yet too often unmemorable whites and reds.

In the main, the whites are made from Chardonnay and the reds from Pinot Noir. The haunting, exotically perfumed, sensuous reds, with coil upon coil of seductive charm unravelling on your palate as the bottle inexorably empties, will be made from Pinot Noir and the stunningly rich, honeyed, nutty, buttery whites that seem to promise an unctuous richness in the palate and yet don't have a trace of sugar in them, will come from Chardonnay. The finest wines make such an impression on those lucky enough to drink them, that for some wine lovers, their life becomes consumed with an obsession to find the next great Burgundy, but even they, employing all their knowledge and passion, will still experience more failures than triumphs.

Good vineyards abound in Burgundy but they have never been numerous enough to satisfy world demand. By the Middle Ages the fame of the wines had spread across northern Europe. Today, the wines have never been more famous or sought after, both red and white Burgundy being held up as the greatest examples of what the Pinot Noir and Chardonnay grapes can achieve. All too frequently demand has outstripped supply and the wines have been too easy to sell, regardless of quality.

In a region where most proprietors own only small plots of land and the majority – except in the Côte de Nuits and Côte de Beaune – are happy to sell their grapes to co-operatives or merchants and pocket the easy profit in both good and less good years, the talented, committed grower who bottles his own wine needs seeking out. Nonetheless, the modern quality revival is being led by a growing band of vineyard owners generally producing small amounts of a dozen or more different wines. Every year new star producers appear and every year the chance of encountering memorable wines from Burgundy becomes greater.

Oz Clarke

The Chambertin-Clos de Bèze Grand Cru shown here is one of Burgundy's top red wine vineyards. Along with Gevrey-Chambertin's other world-famous Grands Crus, it lies south of the village on an east-facing, gently sloping hillside.

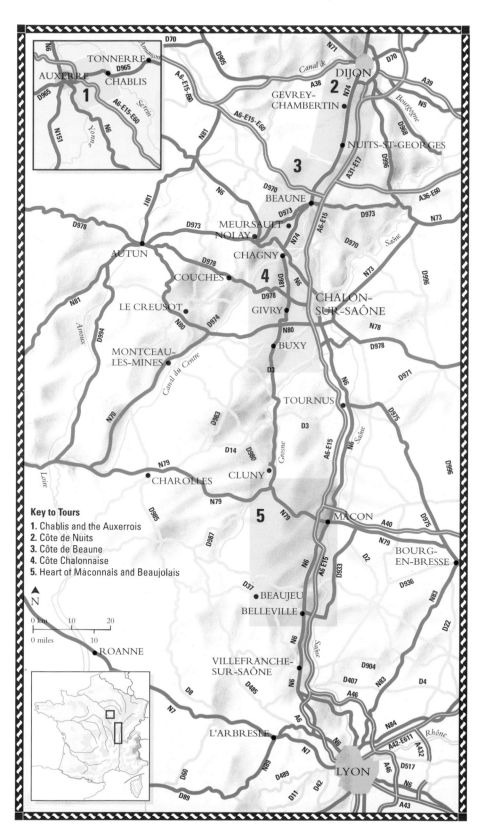

N6
TONNERRE
D965
AUXERRE
CHABLIS
1
D965
A6-E15-E60
Serein
N151
N6
Yonne
D70
Armançon
D905
A6-E15-E60
A38
DIJON
N71
D70
Canal de
GEVREY-
CHAMBERTIN
2
N74
A39
N5
Bourgogne
A6-E15-E60
N81
D968
NUITS-ST-GEORGES
3
A31-E17
D996
N6
D970
BEAUNE
A36-E60
D973
D973
N73
D978
D973
MEURSAULT
NOLAY
A6-E15
D970
Saône
AUTUN
CHAGNY
N74
D978
COUCHES
4
D981
N6
N73
D996
D978
CHALON-
SUR-SAÔNE
N81
LE CREUSOT
GIVRY
D974
N80
N78
Arroux
D994
N80
BUXY
D978
MONTCEAU-
LES-MINES
Canal du Centre
D3
D971
N6
N70
TOURNUS
D975
D983
D3
Saône
N79
D14
D980
A6-E15
N6
D996
Loire
CHAROLLES
CLUNY
Grosne
Key to Tours
1. Chablis and the Auxerrois
2. Côte de Nuits
3. Côte de Beaune
4. Côte Chalonnaise
5. Heart of Mâconnais and Beaujolais
N79
D985
5
N79
MÂCON
A40
D975
D987
N79
BOURG-
EN-BRESSE
N6
A6-E15
D933
D2
D936
N83
N
D37
BEAUJEU
BELLEVILLE
N6
Saône
D22
0 km   10   20
0 miles   10
ROANNE
VILLEFRANCHE-
SUR-SAÔNE
N6
D904
D407
N83
D4
D8
D485
A46
N7
A6
N84
L'ARBRESLE
A42-E611
Rhône
A432
N7
N6
D60
N89
D517
LYON
A6
N6
D489
D42
D89
D11
A43

5

Wine at a Glance

Burgundy's production (excluding Beaujolais) is less than a quarter of that of Bordeaux. Many of the smallest appellations in France are found here; vineyards are tiny and often further fragmented by multiple ownership. The region's reputation rests on its Grands Crus, which account for just one per cent of the wine produced, and its Premiers Crus, a further 11 per cent. But from this minuscule power-base, Burgundy manages to produce the kind of wines that are emulated by producers worldwide.

The brilliantly coloured Côte de Nuits-Villages (left) will deepen with 3–5 years' age, while the pale gold Chassagne-Montrachet becomes deeper and fuller over a decade.

Grape Varieties

There are four main grape varieties: Pinot Noir is used almost exclusively for red wine, except for Beaujolais which is made from Gamay. Chardonnay is used for the great white Burgundies. Aligoté is the other main white grape.

Pinot Noir

Of all the classic grape varieties Pinot Noir is the most tricky. Its thin skin makes it prone to rot and it must be cropped to the minimum. The colour of the wine is never very deep, nor is it excessively structured. Its delicate flavours can be swamped by too much oak. But when it is great – in the Grands and Premiers Crus of the

Gamay

Pinot Noir

Côte d'Or – it is glorious. Flavoured with summer fruits – blackcurrant, raspberry, strawberry and cherry – with hints of coffee and chocolate, Pinot Noir gets more gamy, complex, spicy and sensual with age. A ripe, balanced Pinot Noir wine can keep as long as any other red. It also makes a delicious rosé.

Gamay

The grape of Beaujolais. The granite hills of the Beaujolais-Villages region transform the rather ordinary Gamay into an immensely quaffable wine, abundantly, seductively fruity

without being sweet, and mouth-filling while light in structure. It should be drunk young. Blend it with one third Pinot Noir and you have Bourgogne-Passe-Tout-Grains.

Chardonnay

The world's most popular white grape is hardy, can be cropped at quite a high level and produces a round wine with a rich, fat mouthfeel and good affinity for oak. It ripens easily, and so there are few 'bad' Chardonnay vintages. In Chablis the wine is taut and steely, while in the Côte d'Or it has more depth and

Chardonnay

richness with oak flavours – these wines last well. In the Mâconnais it is lush, succulent and matures early.

Aligoté

Used only for generic wines, where it will state Aligoté on the label, this variety has fallen out of favour – a Chardonnay wine will sell for a higher price. It can be thin and tart, but from a good vineyard, such as at Bouzeron in the Côte Chalonnaise, it is more lemon-tangy and most refreshing, but must be drunk young.

Aligoté

Other Varieties

In the Yonne there is some Sauvignon Blanc at St-Bris producing crisp, herbal, dry whites, and the few reds, such as Irancy, may contain some César. Elsewhere, Pinots Blanc and Gris yield wines with higher alcohol but less acidity than Chardonnay.

Understanding Red and White Burgundy

You can learn something about a wine simply by looking at the bottle – the shape and colour of a traditional Burgundy bottle is used around the world.

Lead capsules used to be common, especially for fine bottles of Burgundy, but EU regulations now require capsules to be made of tin foil or plastic.

The level of fill usually comes to just below the bottom of the cork, but the gap – or ullage – will slowly increase with age, though it should still remain small.

The classic Burgundy bottle has low-sloping shoulders. The majority of Chardonnay and Pinot Noir produced elsewhere around the world imitates this shape.

A neck label for the vintage saves the producer the cost of reprinting the main label each year. However, if it comes off at some stage, the capsule must be removed to see the year stamped on the cork.

Bottles of white Burgundy are often a distinct yellow-green colour known as *feuille morte*, or dead leaf – a colour now used in the New World for Chardonnay.

Bottles of red Burgundy are usually made from an olive green glass – a heavier, darker bottle offers marginally greater protection against damaging light and heat.

The celebrated wine village of Meursault is home to Perrières, one of the most famous Premier Cru vineyards.

A large village AC such as this one means large variations in quality.

Small, quality growers such as Mortet do much to restore this famous wine's reputation.

WINE CLASSIFICATIONS

There are five levels of classification in Burgundy:
General regional appellations Bourgogne is the most basic level covering red, white and rosé wines that do not qualify for one of the higher ACs. There are massive differences in style and quality. Sometimes Bourgogne is used with a more specific geographical description, for example, Bourgogne-Côte Chalonnaise. Bourgogne Passe-Tout-Grains and the very basic Bourgogne Grand Ordinaire are blends of Pinot Noir and inferior Gamay. Crémant de Bourgogne is an AC for sparkling wine made by the Champagne method.
Specific regional appellations These wines are blends from a particular area, for example, Chablis.

Village appellations Each village has its vineyards legally defined, and in the Côte d'Or those with no special reputation, which do not qualify for the higher levels of Premier or Grand Cru, are usually sold under the village name. The wine may be blended from more than one vineyard within the village (and usually from more than one grower, in the case of a merchant's wine). There is a growing move toward adding the name of a lieu-dit or 'stated place' on the label with the village name, although the lettering must be half the size of that of the village name. In Beaujolais there are ten separate villages called Crus whose names appear on the label without any reference to Beaujolais.
Premier Cru (First Growth) Despite the name these are, in fact, the

second best vineyard sites in Burgundy. Even so, they include some of the region's finest wines. They are classified by both village and vineyard name, for example, Gevrey-Chambertin, Combe-aux-Moines. A few vineyards, such as Clos des Mouches (Beaune), are well known in their own right, but a wine from an obscure Premier Cru vineyard, or sourced from more than one, will add just 'Premier Cru' after the village name.
Grand Cru (Great Growth) This is the top level of wine. All Grands Crus are allowed to use their name on the label without the village name. With the exception of Corton in the Côte de Beaune, all the red Grands Crus are in the Côte de Nuits. All the white Grands Crus are in the Côte de Beaune and Chablis.

HOW BURGUNDY WORKS

Before the French Revolution land in Burgundy was owned by the Church and the aristocracy, leased out in small parcels to individual growers, usually on a share-cropping basis. The grower would harvest the grapes, vinify the wine, and then sell it to a merchant or négociant, who would then blend it with wine from other parcels, mature, bottle and eventually sell it.

After 1793 the role of the merchant grew in importance. Individual vineyard parcels became more fragmented as one generation succeeded another, since French law insisted that inheritance be shared equally among all the heirs. For this reason nearly all Burgundian vineyards (or *climats*) are in multiple ownership.

The 20th century has seen two important changes. In 1936 the vineyards were officially classified for the first time with the potential of the site rather than the quality of the wine deciding the rank. The second innovation was the formation of co-operatives, jointly owned by local growers. Most have an excellent reputation, and as well as selling wines under their own labels, supply the local négociants with bulk wine.

How to Choose Burgundy

Reading the label reveals much about the quality of a wine. The most important name is the producer – a good one usually makes reliable wine at all levels year in, year out, from his top wines down to his basic Bourgogne. Next comes the level of the wine: in most cases a Grand Cru will be better than a Premier Cru, and so on. Naturally, prices will follow this hierarchy. Least important, particularly for white wines, is the vintage. With today's techniques for avoiding rot and controlling the wine-making, there are no longer 'bad' vintages – just good and better wines, just early-maturing styles and wines which will need to be kept.

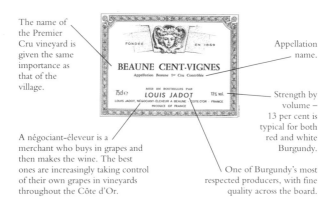

The name of the Premier Cru vineyard is given the same importance as that of the village.

A négociant-éleveur is a merchant who buys in grapes and then makes the wine. The best ones are increasingly taking control of their own grapes in vineyards throughout the Côte d'Or.

Appellation name.

Strength by volume – 13 per cent is typical for both red and white Burgundy.

One of Burgundy's most respected producers, with fine quality across the board.

GLOSSARY

Acidity Important component of wine that gives it its freshness and is crucial to its balance and the impression it makes on the palate.
Botrytis Cinerea Fungus responsible for noble rot as well as the undesirable grey rot.
Cave French for cellar.
Cave Co-opérative A common organization in French wine areas. It caters for the grape grower who has no means of making his own wine.
Champagne Method Process that includes a second FERMENTATION in the bottle – mandatory for the finest sparkling wines.
Chaptalization Addition of sugar to ensure a complete alcoholic FERMENTATION, which adds a degree or two of extra alcohol.
Climat An individual vineyard site, often very small. Generally less specific than LIEU-DIT.
Clos French term for a vineyard that was or still is enclosed by a wall. Most clos are in Burgundy.
Commune Village and its surrounding area – the smallest political division in France.
Côte French for slope or hill. Used in the name of many wine areas.
Crémant French sparkling wine made by the Champagne method.
Cru French term literally meaning growth and used to designate a

single vineyard. In Beaujolais denotes the ten villages with their own appellations.
Égrappage French for destalking.
Élevage Handling and maturing of the wine after fermentation and before bottling.
Extract Soluble substances in wine that influence structure and flavour.
Fermentation (alcoholic) Conversion of grape sugar into alcohol and carbon dioxide with the aid of yeasts.
Filtration Removal of solids and impurities from wine before bottling. The implication for quality and stability is currently one of the most contentious issues in wine production.
Fining Clarifying wine by the addition of a coagulant such as egg-whites to remove soluble particles. Part of the same debate as FILTRATION.
Lieu-Dit Named vineyard site that may also be a Premier or Grand Cru vineyard name (or refer only to a more specific part of one).
Macération Carbonique Wine-making method adapted for Beaujolais: whole berries are fermented within a closed container to extract maximum colour and fruit but minimum tannin.
Malolactic Fermentation Secondary fermentation that converts the harsher malic acid into the softer

lactic acid. Mandatory for red wines, it is also common in Burgundy for whites.
Mesoclimate/Microclimate Mesoclimate refers to the climate of a distinct geographical area, microclimate to conditions surrounding the vine.
Must Mulch of grape juice, skins, pulp and pips.
Négociant-Éleveur Merchant who buys grapes or just-fermented wine, then undertakes ÉLEVAGE and further operations. May also own vineyards.
Nouveau The earliest released Beaujolais in November each year; also the poorest in quality.
Oak Wood used for wine casks. It imparts important flavours during fermentation and aging.
Organic Viticulture Avoidance of chemical fertilizers, herbicides and pesticides and certain additives in the vineyard and wine-making.
Tannin Substance derived from grape skins, stems and pips as well as oak barrels; important to wine structure and aging potential. Its quantity and quality determine the sensation in the mouth.
Terroir Unique physical environment of a vineyard, comprising the soil, elevation, orientation and climate.
Vieilles Vignes Refers to 'old vines' which can give concentrated wine.

Understanding Beaujolais

Fruity, gulpable Beaujolais comes in three categories. Basic Beaujolais – including Nouveau – is made for early drinking and accounts for half the harvest. Beaujolais-Villages is much better quality and needs drinking within two years, while the Beaujolais Crus can retain their fruit intensity and add a silky texture with three or more years' bottle age.

A lighter olive green glass than usual is used – protection from the light is unnecessary since the wine spends little time in bottle before being consumed.

The classic Burgundy bottle shape is also used in Beaujolais.

The most important producer name in Beaujolais.

One of 10 Crus – no reference to Beaujolais is necessary on the label.

An individual vineyard or lieu-dit.

Crémant de Bourgogne

Crémant de Bourgogne provides some of the best French sparkling wine outside Champagne, using the best two grapes of that region, Pinot Noir and Chardonnay.

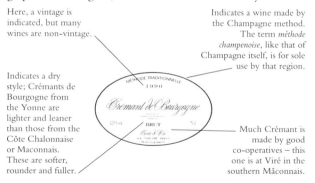

Here, a vintage is indicated, but many wines are non-vintage.

Indicates a dry style; Crémants de Bourgogne from the Yonne are lighter and leaner than those from the Côte Chalonnaise or Maconnais. These are softer, rounder and fuller.

Indicates a wine made by the Champagne method. The term *méthode champenoise*, like that of Champagne itself, is for sole use by that region.

Much Crémant is made by good co-operatives – this one is at Viré in the southern Mâconnais.

VINTAGES
Vintages throughout Burgundy differ greatly because of huge variations in climatic conditions.
1996 Healthy ripe grapes, despite a seesaw growing season. There will be some excellent reds and whites, especially where yields are low.
1995 Small quantities of very good and consistent reds for keeping. Also some very good, concentrated and ageworthy whites.
1994 An irregular vintage for reds, resulting in soft wines that will be ready soon. Better in the Côte de Nuits, southern Côte de Beaune and Côte Chalonnaise than in Volnay, Pommard, Beaune and Savigny. The whites are only average and for drinking soon as well; rather dull Chablis.
1993 Much very good red that will merit keeping. Many whites are lean and for early drinking, but the best have the concentration to support the acidity and will keep. Chablis is dull, leaner and for drinking soon.
1992 A year for soft reds that are pleasant rather than great and for drinking soon. Start to drink the good to very good whites, which are both ample and fruity. Unfortunately, this quality doesn't extend to the large quantity of unexciting Chablis.
1991 In the shadow of the great 90s. There are some very good reds still developing. Dull whites.
1990 A great year – the reds deserve further keeping. Very good whites in all areas and ready now.
1989 The reds are rich and ready to drink. The whites are richer but with less grip than the 90s and can be drunk now.
1988 Austere reds with great elegance. Slow developing, they are only just ready and will repay further keeping. Whites are similarly austere but only the best have much interest.
1987 Some good wines but they should be drunk soon. Many of the whites are past their best.
1986 Reds were weak in the Côte de Beaune and, although better elsewhere, should be drunk up soon. Whites are rich, alcoholic and often unbalanced.
1985 A very good year. Some wines evolved too quickly but there is plenty of fruit and the best will last well. The whites were fine and will continue to last.
Older vintages Despite the rot, a few 83s are very impressive. 1978 was saved by a hot September and the top wines are good. Only a few 1976 reds have maintained their early vigour. Despite hail, 1971 is a classic and the wines have aged impressively.
Other good years 1969 66 64 62 61 59 57 55 53 49 48 47 45.

Regional Food

Burgundy's green rolling hills produce a stunning range of produce for the cook.

Burgundy is one of the richest and most varied gastronomic regions in France. The local cuisine is whole and hearty – it has not lost its peasant roots – nor has it been emasculated by fads for *minceur* or lean cuisine. It is, above all, a *cuisine de terroir et de saison* (cooking according to locality and season). Every small area of Burgundy has its specialities.

Such bountiful food is the result of a varied and rich landscape that has a temperate climate. In the north and west, there are lush pastures where the dun-coloured Charolais beef cattle graze; the wild mountainous forests of the Morvan are home to wild boar and deer; while the flatlands and waterpools of the Saône basin and the Bresse provide fish and the world-famous Bresse chickens, which have their own *appellation contrôlée*.

On all sides there are rivers. In the Chablis area they flow north to the Seine; beyond the Mâconnais and the Beaujolais they flow west into the Loire; and in the east they flow south to the Rhône. Freshwater fish abound, from *écrevisses* (crayfish) to *sandre* (pike-perch), *anguille* (eel), *tanche* (tench), *truite* (trout) and *brochet* (pike).

There are also wild duck, quail (*caille*), pigeon, pheasant and other game birds, not to mention hare and rabbit. The woodlands yield an abundance of wild mushrooms: *cèpes*, *girolles*, *morilles* and *mousserons*, to mention only a few. The market gardens provide a wide variety of vegetables and fruits, particularly blackcurrants (made into sorbets or the local *crème de cassis*, or blackcurrant liqueur), cherries and walnuts. There is an almost infinite variety of cheese – if you include all the local goat's cheeses (*fromage de chèvre*). And, of course, there are the snails (*escargots*) and frogs' legs (*cuisses de grenouilles*) for which France is so famous.

Dijon is known for two culinary essentials: mustard and *crème de cassis*. The former is spicy and hot, less fiery than the English version and not as sweet as the German or American. The famous Maison Grey-Poupon company founded in 1577 still exists in Dijon. *Crème de cassis* blended with Aligoté (one tablespoonful per glass) makes Kir, named after a priest famous for his efforts in the Resistance. Add *crème de cassis* to Crémant de Bourgogne, the local sparkling wine, and you have Kir Royale.

Buying Food

Throughout Burgundy, as elsewhere in France, a wealth of prepared dishes is found in local *boucheries*, *charcuteries* and *boulangeries/pâtisseries*. The *boucheries* and *charcuteries* sell a huge range of hams (*jambon persillé* is a Burgundian speciality), salamis and sausages, pâtés and terrines, and all sorts of salads, plus *andouillettes* and more ambitious take-away dishes (yes, even *boeuf bourguignon*!) to heat up at home.

Each major town will have at least one *maître fromagier* or specialist cheesemonger selling a mountain of local and not-so-local cheeses. The best Burgundian cheeses include l'Ami du Chambertin and Chaource (both mild fat cheeses); Bleu de Bresse (a mild blue-veined cheese); Cîteaux (a firm, mild cheese made by the monks of the Cîteaux abbey); Époisses (a pungent soft cheese that comes in various preparations); l'Amour de Nuits (similar to Époisses); Gex (similar to Roquefort); Passin (Gruyère-like); St-Florentin (another pungent cheese, so runny it is best sometimes to eat it with a spoon); and Soumaintrain (a soft, quite strong Yonne cheese similar to St-Florentin). There are many other cheeses that can be found only within the region; some may even be produced by only one farm. No one goat's cheese, for the variety is legion, tastes quite like another.

With a picnic, indeed with any meal you buy, you will need bread. The French *baguette* is unequalled, but there is plenty more variety than that. And at the *boulangerie/pâtisserie* there will be a mouthwatering variety of fruit flans and individual tarts for afterwards. Before wine-tasting, buy a bag of *gougères* (cheese-flavoured choux-pastry buns) as they are a delicious way of absorbing the wine.

Of course, every important locality has a market, some taking place weekly, some more frequently. Any French market is a bustling, haggling affair, with a colourful display of goods on sale, from animals, still straining at the leash, to farmhouse cheeses, fruits and vegetables; from local honey and wild mushrooms collected at dawn, to home-cured hams and gnarled, ugly-looking salami-type sausages. Burgundian markets are no exception. Get there early in the morning – although if you arrive late you might get a bargain if someone has a surplus – walk round the whole place once before you get tempted, and look to see where the locals are shopping. If one stand has a queue and its neighbour has no customers, there is probably a good reason.

Eating Out

Restaurants in Burgundy range from grand Michelin three-star establishments, of which there are six in the region, to simple bistros which can be excellent places to stop for lunch. You can pay anything from a modest sum that includes wine to ten times that amount for food alone. It is wise to book, especially for Friday and Saturday evenings and Sunday lunch, which is a favourite time for the French to eat out *en famille*. Service is almost invariably friendly, helpful and, most importantly, knowledgeable.

Visitors to Burgundy are advised to diet before or after – while you are there, indulge yourself!

The region's broad expanses of forest provide a wealth of mushrooms such as these cèpes.

REGIONAL SPECIALITIES

Escargots à la bourguignonne
Snails (a vineyard pest) simmered in wine, then stuffed back in their shells with a parsley- and garlic-flavoured butter.
Quenelles de brochet Poached spoonfuls of pike mousse.
Salade aux foies de volailles
Warm salad with chicken livers.
Oeufs en meurette Eggs poached in a rich red wine sauce. This sauce is also used for fish, ham, meat and chicken.
Ecrevisses à la nage Crayfish served in their cooking stock, sometimes with cream added.
Flammiche A leek flan, sometimes with slivers of bacon.
Pouchouse A selection of freshwater fish stewed with white Burgundy.
Jambon persillé Ham cooked with gelatinous stock, parsley and garlic, set and sliced, a speciality of the Côte d'Or.
Jambon à la lie de vin Ham braised on wine lees.
Lapin rôti Roast rabbit, often served in a rich mustard and cream sauce.
Andouillettes Sausages made with pig's tripe and chitterlings with a strong, earthy flavour.
Coq au vin This ubiquitous dish is a Burgundian classic and all the better for being cooked in red Burgundy on home territory.
Poulet de Bresse These superb chickens are often simply roasted; *en vessie*, the chicken is poached in a pig's bladder with young spring vegetables.
Boeuf bourguignon The classic beef and wine stew made with good red Burgundy.
Charollais beef . Steaks from the prized Charollais beef cattle are often served with a rich red-wine sauce.
Marcassin Young wild boar (*sanglier*), often spit-roasted.

This view of the Chablis Grands Crus looks north-west across the great slope of vines. Bathed in the November afternoon sun, les Grenouilles Grand Cru is in the foreground with Vaudésir, les Preuses (up the slope) and Bougros (down the slope) in the middle distance. The little Serein river at the foot of the slope seems hardly more than a stream and across it are the outskirts of the town of Chablis. Notice how the vines are trained: one cane of last year's wood is left and tied horizontally on the lowest wire. From this cane next year's growth will burst forth and the new cane will be fastened to the upper wire. The almost white Kimmeridgian marly limestone and clay soil is rich in fossilized oyster shells.

The Beaujolais region is packed with vineyards on almost every available piece of land and makes excellent wine touring country.

Touring Burgundy

The Burgundian region is typical of the heart of France in many ways. Wine, though vital to the local economy, is only one of a number of agricultural pursuits and vines are largely confined to the most suitable south-facing sites, where they can do best. Elsewhere cattle meditate quietly in lush pastures, and fields are given over to arable produce: wheat, maize and fodder for animals. Sheep and goats graze on the high ground and in a few corners there is the odd bustle of industry. But away from the few large towns this is a rural landscape.

The main wine town is Beaune. Dijon is the Côte d'Or's administrative capital, Auxerre is that of the Yonne and Mâcon of the Saône-et-Loire. Other important towns are Tournus and Chalon in the central part of the region and Belleville and Villefranche in the Beaujolais region. The small town of Chablis is the focal point of its wine region.

Hotels in Burgundy range from the de luxe to the simply functional, there are bed and breakfast establishments (*chambres d'hôtes*) or you can hire a *gîte*. Hotels are likely to be in the main centres but one of the advantages of more modest accommodation is that is more likely be located in the countryside. Nights will be more peaceful, and you will be able to absorb more of *la Bourgogne profonde*.

Burgundy can be very cold in winter, and even 5°C (41°F) colder up in a *gîte* in the Hautes-Côtes than in the centre of a main town. Naturally the winter is bleak, the countryside less attractive, and the days short. After mid-November, therefore, is a risky time to visit the region. From mid-March to high summer is a good time for wine touring and Burgundy is looking at its best then – the hedgerows are blooming with wild flowers, the birds triumphant in song and the woods and vineyards burgeoning with new growth. In March the vine wakes up from its winter dormancy and the buds are evident; in late April they burst to reveal a small cluster of tiny leaves; and in early June they flower, hopefully in good weather, and the flowers will set into fruit. Throughout this period the growers will be busy, but they may have a few moments for visitors.

Avoid the high summer, between July and September. It can be too hot for serious tasting and the growers will be taking their holidays too. Vintage time from September to mid-October is also not a good time to visit growers. As well as the new wine to be made, bottling of the previous year's crop is often taking place. But nevertheless autumn can be a very attractive time to visit Burgundy. And you can plan your visit to coincide with the annual celebrations at the Hospices de Beaune.

SUMMARY OF TOURS

Chablis and the Auxerrois A tour of the northernmost Burgundy vineyards, which are famous for crisp white wines.

Côte de Nuits An exploration of the northern part of the Côte d'Or, along the 'Route des Grands Crus' between Nuits-St-Georges and Dijon, to sample great red Burgundies.

Côte de Beaune A trip through the varied countryside of the southern Côte d'Or, visiting the many world-famous white wine villages.

Côte Chalonnaise Wine villages south of the Côte d'Or, which are the source of increasingly well-made and good-value Burgundy red and white wines.

Heart of Mâconnais and Beaujolais A tour of two contrasting wines: lush countryside to the west of Mâcon, where the wine villages make white Pouilly-Fuissé, then south to the Cru villages of red Beaujolais.

Chablis and the Auxerrois

The Grand Cru vineyards rise up above the little town of Chablis, nestling in the Serein Valley.

Northern Burgundy is a landscape of weathered hills, lush pasture, cereal fields and only occasional vineyards. Chablis is world famous for its crisp, bone-dry, white wines from Chardonnay, yet the area and its Auxerrois satellites are all that remains from a vast vineyard area that only 150 years ago extended north from Dijon even to the gates of Paris. Vine disease, industrialization, the new railways (enabling cheaper Midi wines to reach the capital) and an economic depression which lasted from 1870 until after World War Two, have all taken their toll and today only the best vineyards in isolated pockets such as Chablis remain.

Chablis is at the northern limit for growing red grapes successfully and so it produces white wine exclusively. Spring frosts are a problem, especially in the Grands Crus in the narrow Serein Valley, which traps the cold air. Antifrost methods used in the vineyards include various types of coal or oil braziers and a system of water pipes which is more expensive to install but cheaper in the long run. When there is a risk of frost the water is turned on and freezes over the vine-bud like an igloo, protecting it from any colder weather that may follow.

The Chablis area is increasing – today there are twice the number of vineyards there were 20 years ago. These are mainly Premiers Crus and basic Chablis, since all the available land for the Grands Crus was planted years ago. Despite this expansion, only south-facing slopes are used for vineyards. The rest of the land is forest, pasture and arable crops.

Oak is a controversial word in Chablis, since there are two distinct schools of thought about its use in making wine. The first, represented by William Fèvre, is that a top Chablis cannot develop in bottle for a decade or more without new oak. The second school, represented by the large firm of J Moreau, abhors the use of wood. Some leading producers, including Raveneau and René and Vincent Dauvissat, use oak barrels (but not new ones), which leaves the wine with only a very slight suggestion of wood.

The Tour

Auxerre, a fine old city beside the river Yonne with a cathedral and streets of gabled houses, makes an excellent point of departure. Leave the centre by crossing the Yonne and heading south on the N6 road toward Avallon. At Champs-sur-Yonne stay on the east side of the river and take the pretty D362 road toward Vincelottes. After a few minutes' driving you reach the Caves de Bailly, one of the area's best

TOUR SUMMARY

The tour begins in the old city of Auxerre, then passes through the Auxerrois vineyards before reaching Chablis, the wine heart of the Yonne *département.*

Distance covered 100km (60 miles).

Time needed 3 hours, excluding detours.

Terrain The tour follows main roads and *départementale* routes that are mainly good and easy to drive. But beware of frost in winter.

Hotels There is a good hotel/restaurant in Chablis itself. Otherwise, Auxerre provides a wide choice.

Restaurants Apart from those in Chablis and Auxerre, there are a number of good local restaurants along the way, at prices to suit all pockets.

SOUGÈRES-SUR-SINOTTE
VILLENEUVE ST SALVES
To Joigny
BLEIGNY LE-CARREAU
LA CHAPELLE LES SOLEINES
VENOY
AUXERRE
NANGIS
QUENNE
AUGY
VAUX
CHITRY
ST-BRIS-LE-VINEUX
CHAMPS-SUR-YONNE
BAILLY
ESCOLIVES-STE-CAMILLE
COULANGES-LA-VINEUSE
VINCELOTTES
IRANCY

To Pontigny
MALIGNY
LA CHAPELLE-VAUPELTEIGNE
FONTENAY-PRÈS-CHABLIS
BEINE
POINCHY
CHABLIS
FLEYS
To Tonnerre
MONTALLERY
CHICHÉE
COURGIS
PRÉHY
ST-CYR-LES-COLONS
PUITS-DE-COURSON
To Avallon

N
0 km   2   4
0 miles   2

Map illustration: Coal and oil braziers are used in the Chablis vineyards as a protection against spring frosts.

producers of Crémant de Bourgogne. Allow about 30 minutes for a visit. At Vincelottes – where the Auberge les Tilleuls makes a good stop for lunch – turn left toward the unspoiled village of Irancy on the D38. The undulating hills here produce Irancy, the Yonne's best red wine. The best producer is Jean-Pierre Colinot.

Long before the August *véraison,* when the leaves of Pinot Noir change from green to black, it is easy to tell the difference between Chardonnay and Pinot Noir. A Pinot Noir leaf is darker, feels thicker, and its two halves are less symmetrical. Another vine grown in the region, Sauvignon Blanc, has a bigger leaf that looks as if it is split into several sections.

From Irancy follow the signs to St-Bris-le-Vineux, the home of Burgundy's only VDQS or Vin Délimité de Qualité Supérieure, the level below Appellation Contrôlée. This white wine from Sauvignon Blanc is not as elegant as Sancerre or Pouilly-Fumé, but the best, such as those made by Jean-Hugues Goisot, are worth trying. Sadly, the more popular Aligoté and Chardonnay (sold as Bourgogne-Côtes d'Auxerre) are beginning to take over the vineyards here as they are more consistent, vintage by vintage, than the Irancy reds and can also be used for the popular local Crémant.

From St-Bris take the D62 road toward Chitry, another important area for Bourgogne-Côtes d'Auxerre; just before Chitry turn left onto a minor road which passes under the motorway to Montallery and Beine, where there is a good restaurant, Le Vaulignot. Turn right onto the D965, the Auxerre to Tonnerre road, and drive to Chablis, passing a large reservoir of water used for spraying the vines when there is a threat of frost in the spring.

Now you are in the Chablis vineyards. Imagine a splayed hand with a small palm and long fingers. The base of the palm covers the Grands Crus, which face the town across the Serein river. The middle of the palm is the town itself, and the tapering fingers are the long valleys, which extend out to Maligny, Beine, Courgis and Tonnerre, and where most of the 40 Premiers Crus are located.

Chablis itself is a small, quiet town but with little charm since most of its old buildings were badly damaged during World War Two. Many leading producers, such as William Fèvre at l'Obédiencerie and la Chablisienne, a co-operative with real class, are based here.

The nearest vineyards are the Grands Crus, which command a magnificent, long, steep, south-west-facing slope opposite the town. To view them properly, cross the Serein and turn left on the D91 road toward Maligny. Stop along the road here and stroll up through the vineyards, where the anti-frost devices can be clearly seen. From east to west the Grands Crus are Blanchots, les Clos, Valmur, les Grenouilles, Vaudésir, les Preuses and Bougros. Below the Grands Crus, halfway between Valmur and les Grenouilles, follow the signs marked 'Panorama' to the edge of the wood at the top of the slopes. The view from here is breathtaking.

The undulating hills around the village of St-Bris-le-Vineux produce Aligoté and Chardonnay, as well as the more traditional Sauvignon Blanc, which is now less popular.

After the Grands Crus, the tour visits the five most reliable Premiers Crus tucked away in the side valleys. Continue to Maligny, passing the Premier Cru Fourchaume on the right. (If you have time, the Abbey at Pontigny is well worth visiting.) Then return to Chablis and take the D965 road toward Fleys and Tonnerre. Beyond the Grands Crus are two more excellent Premiers Crus, Montée de Tonnerre and Mont de Milieu. (From here it is only 9km/ 6 miles to Tonnerre, a pleasant town above the Armançon river overlooked by vineyards.) Another minor detour here would be to head south around the Premier Cru Vaucoupin – the junction is below Mont de Milieu – to the village of Chichée, home of some good growers, including Gilbert Picq.

To visit the remaining top Premiers Crus, return to Chablis and take the D62 road toward Courgis, passing Montmains and beyond it, in the next valley, Vaillons. Again return to Chablis, turn left, and take the direct road back to Auxerre.

Chablis and the Auxerrois Fact File

Auxerre, the capital of the Yonne *département*, has many of the best places to stay and eat. Chablis is hardly more than a large village but is, of course, the centre of the wine area.

Information

BIVB (Chablis-Auxerrois)/ Office du Tourisme
Le Petit Pontigny, 1 rue de Chichée, 89800 Chablis. Tel 03 86 42 80 80; fax 03 86 42 80 16.
As well as being the tourist office, this is the local branch of Burgundy's wine information service or BIVB.

Office du Tourisme
Quai de la République, 89000 Auxerre. Tel 03 86 52 06 19; fax 03 86 51 23 27.

Where to Buy Wine

Most of the local growers are only too happy to sell their wine to you.
Caves de Bailly
Quai de l'Yonne, St-Bris-le-Vineux, 89530 Bailly. Tel 03 86 53 34 00; fax 03 86 53 80 94.
A good sparkling wine specialist.

Le Cellier Chablisien
Rue Jules Rathier, 89800 Chablis. Tel 03 86 42 15 64; fax 03 86 42 82 06.
An excellent selection of wines from promising local growers.

La Chablisienne
8 boulevard Pasteur, 89800 Chablis. Tel 03 86 42 89 89; fax 03 86 42 89 90.
A very good co-operative that makes nearly one-third of all Chablis.

Jean-Pierre Colinot
1 rue des Chariats, 89290 Irancy. Tel & fax 03 86 42 33 25.
Leading producer of red Irancy.

Ghislaine et Jean-Hugues Goisot
30 rue Bienvenu-Martin, 89530 St-Bris-le-Vineux. Tel 03 86 53 35 15; fax 03 86 53 62 03.
Reliable reds and whites from this husband-and-wife team.

Festivals and Events

The annual Chablis wine festival takes place on the fourth Saturday in November. Visitors can taste the latest vintage and other wines. The Fête du Sauvignon at St-Bris-le-Vineux is in mid-November. The local wine brotherhood is called the Piliers Chablisiens.

Where to Stay and Eat

Hôtel Abbaye St-Michel Ⓗ Ⓡ
Montée St-Michel, 89700 Tonnerre. Tel 03 86 55 05 99; fax 03 86 55 00 10. Ⓕ Ⓕ Ⓕ
An expensive *Relais et Châteaux* establishment that was formerly a monastery. Very good – but not brilliant – food and wine list.

Jean-Luc Barnabet Ⓡ
14 quai République, 89000 Auxerre. Tel 03 86 51 68 88; fax 03 86 52 68 33. Ⓕ Ⓕ Ⓕ
Auxerre's best restaurant with a very good wine list.

L'Obédiencerie in the centre of Chablis is the headquarters of William Fèvre, a leading producer.

La Chamaille Ⓡ
Barbotière, 4 route de Boiloup, 89420 Chevannes. Tel 03 86 41 24 80; fax 03 81 41 34 80. Ⓕ Ⓕ
One of the best restaurants in the area, in a 16th-century mansion just south-west of Auxerre. The service is welcoming and the wine list good.

Auberge du Château Ⓗ Ⓡ
85580 Val de Mercy. Tel 03 86 41 60 00; fax 03 86 41 73 28. Ⓕ Ⓕ

South-west of Vincelottes, this former coaching inn is now a restaurant serving good food. There are also 4 comfortable bedrooms.

Hostellerie les Clos Ⓗ Ⓡ
Rue Jules Rathier, 89800 Chablis. Tel 03 86 42 10 63; fax 03 86 42 17 11. Ⓕ Ⓕ
The best place to eat, and the only place to stay, in Chablis itself. Airy, comfortable, modern rooms most of which have views of the garden. There is a very good restaurant with an extensive wine list, seasonal food and efficient service.

Jardin Gourmand Ⓡ
56 boulevard Vauban, 89000 Auxerre. Tel 03 86 51 53 52; fax 03 86 52 33 82. Ⓕ Ⓕ
This is a stylish converted mansion serving good, well-presented food full of original ideas. Good wine list.

Hotel Parc des Maréchaux Ⓗ
6 avenue Foch, 89000 Auxerre. Tel 03 86 51 43 77; fax 03 86 52 21 70. Ⓕ Ⓕ
The elegant rooms of this hotel have been newly renovated. Some of the bedrooms open onto a private park.

Hôtel Relais St-Vincent Ⓗ Ⓡ
89144 Ligny-le-Châtel. Tel 03 86 47 53 38; fax 03 86 47 54 16. Ⓕ Ⓕ
Just north of Maligny, this unpretentious hotel makes a good base in the Chablis area. As well as the restaurant, there is a terrace for eating outside.

Auberge les Tilleuls Ⓗ Ⓡ
89290 Vincelottes. Tel 03 86 42 22 13; fax 03 86 42 23 51. Ⓕ
This is a good place to stop for lunch in the vicinity of Irancy. You can also eat outside in summer. There are 4 bedrooms.

Le Vaulingot Ⓡ
89800 Beine. Tel 03 86 42 48 48. Ⓕ
This is a good simple place to stop for lunch between Auxerre and Chablis.

Wines and Wine Villages

The main wine of the area is Chablis, exclusively white from Chardonnay. Several outlying villages make red and white Bourgogne-Côtes d'Auxerre and other wines.

Beine This is the first village you reach if you are driving to Chablis from the autoroute. The Premiers Crus of Troesmes, Vau Ligneau and Vau de Vey are here.

Bourgogne Côtes-d'Auxerre AC This is the local name for the basic Bourgogne wine. Most of the white comes from Chardonnay and the red from Pinot Noir.

Chablis AC This AC for basic Chablis covers most of the region's vineyards. Straight Chablis should have a light, unassertive fruit for delicious drinking at only a few years old. Some producers are now experimenting with oak aging. The small town of Chablis now includes the hamlets of Fyé, Milly and Poinchy. It is the hub, naturally enough, of the AC and most of Chablis's main growers and merchants, as well as the co-operative and the best local shops, are here. All the Grands Crus lie within its boundaries and most of the best Premiers Crus are nearby.
Best producers: BILLAUD-SIMON, *Pascal Bouchard, la Chablisienne,* RENÉ ET VINCENT DAUVISSAT, JEAN-PAUL DROIN, WILLIAM FÈVRE, *Laroche, Long-Depaquit, Louis Michel, J Moreau, Louis Pinson, Gilbert Picq,* JEAN-MARIE RAVENEAU.

Chablis Grand Cru AC The 7 Chablis Grands Crus face south-west across the town. Here, in this long sweep of vineyards, the combination of soil, aspect and mesoclimate are at their best. From east to west the Grands Crus are: Blanchots (13.1ha), les Clos (27ha), Valmur (12.9ha), les Grenouilles (10ha), Vaudésir (16.2ha), les Preuses (11.9ha) and Bougros (15.9ha). Les Clos is generally regarded as the best, followed by Valmur. Both are racy, elegant wines.

Vaudésir is firmer and fuller, even richer, as is Preuses, which can be a little heavy. The upper part of Bougros produces wines similar to Preuses (not surprisingly, as they are adjacent) but the wines from the lower part are considered less stylish, as are those from Blanchots and les Grenouilles.
Best producers: *See Chablis AC.*

Chablis Premier Cru AC There are 40 Premiers Crus but many sell under a neighbouring, more famous name, effectively rationalizing the list into 17 Premiers Crus. The best of these are Fourchaume, Vaillons, Montée de Tonnerre, Montmains, Mont de Milieu and Côte de Léchet (in rough order of precedence) followed by Vaucoupin, les Forneaux, Beauroy, Mélinots, Vosgros and Vau de Vey.
Best producers: *See Chablis AC.*

La Chapelle-Vaupelteigne Facing the Premiers Crus of Fourchaume and l'Homme Mort, this village has the highest ratio of Premier Cru to basic Chablis land. The chapel dates from AD 903.

Chichée On the left bank of the Serein, Chichée with its medieval buildings is still charmingly unspoilt. Vaucoupin, Vosrigaut and Vosgros are the local Premiers Crus.

Chitry Along with St-Bris, Chitry is another centre of Bourgogne-Côtes d'Auxerre this time for Chardonnay. Both this and Aligoté are made into Crémant de Bourgogne by the nearby Caves de Bailly.

Coulanges-la-Vineuse Coulanges is a centre for red Bourgogne-Côtes d'Auxerre made from Pinot Noir. The reds are even lighter than Irancy's.

Courgis This picturesque village contains the Premiers Crus Côte de Cuissy, les Beauregards, les Landes et Verjuts and Chaume de Talvat. Most of the local growers belong to the co-operative.

Épineuil The Épineuil vineyards are on a hill above the Armançon river near Tonnerre. A few brave locals have started to rejuvenate the area and plant Pinot Noir. So far, the most notable wines are the rosés.

Fleys There is a fine Renaissance church at Fleys as well as the Premiers Crus Mont de Milieu, Morein, Côte de Près-Girots and les Fourneaux.

Irancy AC This pretty village overlooking the Yonne is the centre for Pinot Noir in the area. This is very definitely a light wine and, in lesser vintages and from lesser producers, can be stringy and rustic, especially if the local César grape is also used.
Best producers: *Colinot.*

Maligny The Kimmeridgian limestone soil found in the heart of Chablis gives way here to the less perfectly balanced Portlandian version (which is why there are no Premiers Crus here). Purists would like the Chablis vineyards restricted to Kimmeridgian soil but, not surprisingly, the Maligny growers are in the expansionist camp.

Petit Chablis AC These are the least well-sited vineyards in Chablis. Over the next few years vineyards may either be promoted to full Chablis or downgraded to white Bourgogne AC.

Sauvignon-de-St-Bris VDQS St-Bris-le-Vineux is the only place Sauvignon Blanc can be grown in Burgundy, hence the wine is classified as VDQS rather than AC. Rather dull, the wine is now out of favour, since it is difficult to sell and cannot be used for the local Crémant.
Best producers: *Goisot.*

Fixin is the northernmost quality wine village in the Côte de Nuits. The fine 12th-century church, with its typically Burgundian multi-coloured, tiled steeple, was once part of a monastery. Its chapter house used to be in the foreground but the land has since become one of Fixin's most important Premier Cru vineyards, Clos du Chapitre. The church has since been deconsecrated and is now an excellent wine cellar. Behind the church leading up to the wooded ridge are the protected, well-drained slopes of two more Premiers Crus, les Hervelets and les Arvelets. All this is Pinot Noir territory. Fixin does make a little white wine, but the top vineyards produce almost exclusively red.

Côte de Nuits

One of the Côte de Nuits' narrowest points is at the Clos des Argillières, a top Nuits-St-Georges Premier Cru.

Map illustrations: (above) a traditional Burgundian silver tastevin; (centre) de Vogüé's medieval courtyard at Chambolle-Musigny; (below) the village sign at Morey-St-Denis.

TOUR SUMMARY

The tour begins and ends in Nuits-St-Georges, commercial capital of the region, and includes two detours up into the scenic Hautes-Côtes.

Distance covered 60km (35 miles).

Time needed 3½ hours, excluding detours.

Terrain In order to get really close to the top vineyards, some of the tour is on very minor roads which can be extremely muddy in winter.

Hotels Dijon and Nuits-St-Georges have the most choice and at a wide range of prices, but there are hotels in the wine villages too.

Restaurants There are good restaurants in Vosne, Flagey, Chambolle, Gevrey and Marsanny as well as at Marey-lès-Fussey up in the hills. Or shop in Nuits for a picnic and drive up into the Hautes-Côtes.

The Côte de Nuits is the greatest stretch of Pinot Noir vineyard in the world, containing 23 out of the 24 Côte d'Or red Burgundy Grands Crus (the exception is Corton in the Côte de Beaune). These great vineyards run in an almost unbroken line from Vosne-Romanée north to Gevrey-Chambertin, and the main part of the tour follows this Route des Grands Crus.

The Côte de Nuits differs from the Côte de Beaune, the southern half of the Côte d'Or, in a number of ways. First, the slope is narrower and steeper, the aspect is more directly east than south-east and the soil, essentially limestone, is a harder and older rock. And it is almost entirely a red wine area. Here, the wines of Burgundy are at their most powerful and long-lasting, slower to come to full maturity, but developing into mellow, complex and concentrated wines. At the top of the slope, the soil is almost entirely weathered rock, meagre in nutrients, exposed to the wind. At the bottom, the slope runs out, there is more clay, and the drainage is less efficient. So it is in mid-slope, where aspect and soil are at their optimum, that the best vineyards are found.

The Tour

The large Nuits-St-Georges appellation divides neatly into two parts, north and south of the river Meuzin, which runs through the town. The tour starts by visiting the southern part, where the Côte de Nuits finally peters out and the Côte de Beaune takes over.

From Nuits-St-Georges take the D8 road south-west toward Chaux, and after only a couple of hundred metres, before it climbs up into the hills, turn left into a small road that passes through the vineyards. On the slopes to the right lie some of Nuits' Premiers Crus – les Pruliers, les Roncières, les Porrets-St-Georges, les Cailles and, finally, les St-Georges itself, Nuits' finest vineyard – all producing full, firm, rich and quite robust wines that repay keeping. Follow the road back round to the main N74 and continue southward.

This is now the commune of Prémeaux-Prissey, but the wines are still part of the Nuits-St-Georges appellation. The main road has climbed diagonally up the slope and here, exceptionally, lies a Premier Cru vineyard, les Grandes Vignes, on the 'wrong', that is, east, side of the road. The Premiers Crus above the road are les Forêts, aux Corvées, les Argillières, Clos l'Arlot, and, once through the village, Clos de la Maréchale, in the sole ownership of Faiveley, an excellent Nuits merchant and grower. The growers Arlot, Confuron-Meunier and Rion are all based in Prémeaux and are excellent places to visit.

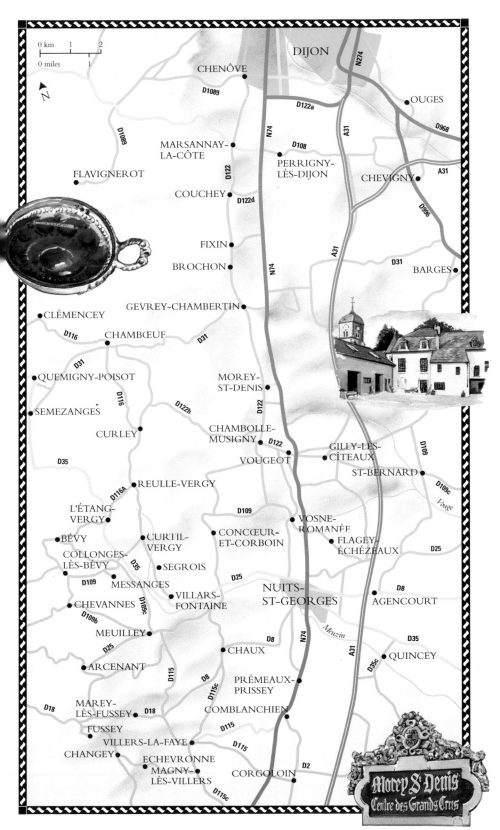

0 km   1   2
0 miles   1

N

DIJON

CHENÔVE

D1089

OUGES

D122a

D968

N274

A31

MARSANNAY-
LA-CÔTE

D108

PERRIGNY-
LÈS-DIJON

CHEVIGNY

A31

FLAVIGNEROT

D1089

D122

N74

D996

COUCHEY

D122d

FIXIN

BROCHON

A31

N74

D31

BARGES

GEVREY-CHAMBERTIN

CLÉMENCEY

CHAMBŒUF

D116

D31

QUEMIGNY-POISOT

D31

MOREY-
ST-DENIS

SEMEZANGES

D116

CURLEY

D122h

D122

CHAMBOLLE-
MUSIGNY

D122

GILLY-LÈS-
CÎTEAUX

D109

D35

VOUGEOT

ST-BERNARD

D109c

REULLE-VERGY

D116A

Vouge

L'ÉTANG-
VERGY

D109

VOSNE-
ROMANÉE

BÉVY

CURTIL-
VERGY

CONCŒUR-
ET-CORBOIN

FLAGEY-
ÉCHÉZEAUX

D25

COLLONGES-
LÈS-BÉVY

D35

SEGROIS

D109

MESSANGES

D25

D8

CHEVANNES

D109c

VILLARS-
FONTAINE

NUITS-
ST-GEORGES

AGENCOURT

D109b

MEUILLEY

D25

CHAUX

D8

N74

Meuzin

D35

QUINCEY

A31

D35c

ARCENANT

D115

D8

D115c

PRÉMEAUX-
PRISSEY

MAREY-
LÈS-FUSSEY

D18

D18

COMBLANCHIEN

D18

FUSSEY

D115

VILLERS-LA-FAYE

D115

CHANGEY

ECHEVRONNE

D2

MAGNY-
LÈS-VILLERS

CORGOLOIN

D115c

Morey St Denis
Centre des Grands Crus

South of Clos de la Maréchale there are fewer vineyards and more quarries and at Corgoloin the Côte de Nuits comes to an end. The villages of Comblanchien, Corgoloin and the Prissey part of Prémeaux use the Côte de Nuits-Villages appellation. In Comblanchien squeeze between the blocks of stone and other rocky debris and take the D115 up into the hills to Villers-la-Faye, passing more quarries on the way.

You will notice a difference between these Hautes-Côtes vineyards up in the hills and those down below on the Côte: the vines are planted further apart and are trained higher. There are three reasons for this. The first is economic, the second is to make mechanical harvesting easier, and the third is to avoid the dangers of frost. The grapes never ripen so easily here and the soil is not as good, but in hotter summers some very decent wines can be made.

From Villers-la-Faye it is a short detour to the excellent grower Jayer-Gilles at Magny-lès-Villers. Continue on to Marey-lès-Fussy where the Maison des Hautes-Côtes makes a convenient lunch stop. Along the road, as well as vines, there are fields of blackcurrant bushes, used locally to produce the liqueur *crème de cassis*. Then return via Chaux to Nuits-St-Georges. Stop near the edge of the escarpment to take in the view. The Premiers Crus you passed earlier on in the tour lie below. In the distance is the Forêt de Citeaux and the old Cistercian abbey, so important in the history of the local vines and wines. To the left, beyond the town of Nuits, the vineyards stretch toward the city of Dijon.

The Domaine des Clos des Langres at Corgoloin is the southernmost estate in the Côte de Nuits.

This completes the shorter, southern, part of the tour, so before continuing north to see the great Grand Cru vineyards, perhaps a short break in Nuits to visit one of the local wine establishments would be welcome. Faiveley, Robert Chevillon and Henri Gouges all welcome visitors by appointment.

Then, from the centre of Nuits take the D25 west toward Meuilley and Arcenant. After only a few hundred metres, make a detour to the right around the back of an Inter-Marché supermarket and take the little road through the vineyards to the north. The road passes between the flatter vineyards lower down the slope, which use the village appellation, and the steeper ones on the slope to the left, which are more of Nuits' Premiers Crus – this time aux Bousselots, aux Chaignots, aux Vignes-Rondes, aux Murgers, with above it les Damodes, and, finally, on the communal boundary with Vosne-Romanée, les Boudots. The wines from the Nuits' vineyards approaching the Vosne-Romanée border become progressively less like the usual sturdy Nuits-St-Georges and closer to the more elegant Vosne-Romanée. Les Boudots is very much a Vosne-Romanée wine in Nuits-St-Georges clothing! A righthand fork will send you down between the Premiers Crus of Chaumes and Clos de Réas into the main square of the village of Vosne-Romanée.

Vosne-Romanée has more good wine producers per square metre than any other village in Burgundy and even perhaps on earth: Arnoux, Cathiard, Confuron-Cotétidot, Engel, Forey, Grivot, various Gros, various Jayers and various Mugnerets, not to mention the world-famous domaines of Leroy and Romanée-Conti. In this modest little village there is majesty within walking distance and magic in the cellars around you.

Up the slope behind the houses are the Grands Crus producing some of the world's best red wines. To reach them, face the *mairie* in the main square, take the lefthand fork and then the third little road up the slope. On the way, the road passes the gunmetal-painted shutters of Domaine de la Romanée-Conti, the largest owner of Vosne's Grands Crus. Once in the vineyards, stop at the next junction, near the stone cross.

This well-drained slope, lying at 250–300m (820–1000ft) with a perfect east and south-east exposure, is revered by many as some of the holiest wine real estate in the world. The soil is limestone, mixed with gravel, clay and sometimes sand, and the vineyards are sheltered from the west and the north by the trees at the top of the slope.

Behind the cross lies tiny, gently sloping Romanée-Conti, surrounded on three sides by a low stone wall, with the even smaller la Romanée Grand Cru above it. At less than 1ha in extent, la Romanée is the smallest individual

The view from la Tâche Grand Cru over Vosne-Romanée and the flat plain beyond is stupendous.

appellation in France. On the left is Grande Rue, a narrow strip of vines, with la Tâche beyond it. On the right, up the slope, is the steeper Richebourg Grand Cru, with below it the largest Vosne Grand Cru, Romanée-St-Vivant. It's worth walking up the slope between Romanée-Conti and Grande Rue.

Take the road between Richebourg and Romanée-St-Vivant to the next junction in front of les Suchots, one of Vosne's top Premiers Crus. For another short detour into the pretty hills, turn left and drive up between the two halves of the aux Brûlées Premier Cru (les Beaux-Monts, another Premier Cru, is above it on the right). After a couple of kilometres the road flattens out and there are more Hautes-Côtes vineyards. The soil here is hardly more than broken-up rock, not the lush pasture found further south in the Hautes-Côtes around Marey-lès-Fussey. If you have time, it's worth continuing as far as Concoeur.

Retrace your route downhill to the junction with les Suchots. Take the next road left between the two halves of les Suchots and then into the large Échézeaux Grand Cru. Further on, to the right, is the much smaller Grands-Échézeaux which is supposed to have acquired its name not because the wine is grander, but because the rows of vines are longer. Confusingly, these two Grands Crus are technically within the commune of Flagey – a village to the east across the main N74 and the railway line and completely cut off from its vineyards. From the Échézeaux vineyards you have a good view of the high stone wall surrounding the Clos de Vougeot Grand Cru and its famous château, which is 2.75km (1¾ miles) long. Vougeot is probably the best-known example of a 'clos', a French term for a walled vineyard. As the road passes the wall, the source of the great Musigny Grand Cru, a red wine of the utmost complexity, fragrance and harmony, lies on the left.

All the vineyards belonging to the Domaine de la Romanée-Conti are marked with a stone cross.

Follow the wall round as far as the entrance to the vineyard and the château, which is home to the Confrérie des Chevaliers du Tastevin, Burgundy's biggest wine fraternity. It's worth going inside just to see the huge 14th-century wine-press that was used by the Cistercian monks. At 52ha Clos de Vougeot is the largest Grand Cru in the Côte de Nuits. Not surprisingly, over such a large area, which starts almost at the top of the slope and descends as far as the flat land by the N74, there are important variations in soil structure, aspect and drainage. Add to this the complex land ownership that is typical of so much of Burgundy (Clos de Vougeot is split into 100 parcels among 80 different owners), and it is no wonder the quality of the wine can be so variable.

Having visited the château, return to the edge of the Musigny Grand Cru and continue northward, passing above les Amoureuses, one of Chambolle-Musigny's best Premiers Crus. At the junction, turn left in the direction of the village of Chambolle. In high summer it is very noticeable that the foliage on the vines here is lighter and yellower in colour than elsewhere along the Côte. This is due to the higher proportion of active limestone in the soil and explains why Chambolle's wines are the most delicate and elegant in the Côte de Nuits.

The 16th-century church in the village stands apart from its bell-tower and outside it are two venerable old lime trees, also dating, it is believed, from the time of the Renaissance. The medieval courtyard and cellars belonging to the Comte Georges de Vogüé, owner of most of the Musigny Grand Cru, are well worth visiting. At the bottom of the village are the domaine and cellars of Ghislaine Barthod. At the higher end of the village are Georges Roumier and the somewhat severe-looking Ch. de Chambolle belonging to the Mugnier family. Unless you want to make another detour into the hills, drive back down the east side of the village – perhaps stopping at the simple bistro of Le Chambolle Musigny – and out along the D122, the Route des Grands Crus, north to Morey-St-Denis.

Here, on the slope, the Grands Crus begin again. Bonnes-Mares lies mostly in the commune of Chambolle-Musigny, but overlaps slightly into Morey-St-Denis. The next Grands Crus along this road are Clos de Tart and Clos des Lambrays. On the north side of the village also are Clos-St-Denis and, perhaps best of all, Clos de la Roche, right on the boundary with Gevrey-Chambertin.

The village of Vougeot lies below Chambolle-Musigny's Premier Cru, les Amoureuses.

Most of Morey-St-Denis' best growers, such as Robert Groffier and Perrot-Minot, are located either along this road, or in Morey's Grande Rue, which runs down to the N74 main road. Dujac, another excellent Morey grower, is located just off the Grande Rue at the bottom of the village. Morey-St-Denis is neither as fragrantly delicious as Chambolle, nor as rich and concentrated as Gevrey-Chambertin, and there are an impossible number of tiny Premiers Crus. But the wine can be good value.

Continue along the Route des Grands Crus through the village to the Place du Monument, the War Memorial, where the lefthand road leads a short way up to a quarry. From here there is an exceptional view of the vineyards and the plain beyond. If Mont Blanc is visible in the distance – look slightly to the right for the glint of the snow – it is supposed to signify rain the next day. Continue north along the Route des Grands Crus toward Gevrey which, like Vosne, has a great cluster of Côte de Nuits' Grands Crus.

The first Gevrey vineyard above the road on the left is a Premier Cru, aux Combottes, but this is quickly followed by a succession of Grands Crus: Latricières-Chambertin,

Chambertin, Chambertin Clos-de-Bèze and Mazis-Chambertin (above which is Ruchottes-Chambertin). Working north from Morey on the righthand side are the Grands Crus Charmes-Chambertin, Mazoyères-Chambertin (whose owners can bottle their wine as Charmes, and most do so), Griottes-Chambertin and Chapelle-Chambertin. In 1848, followed subsequently by many other Côte d'Or wine villages, the mayor of Gevrey decided to add the name Chambertin, the commune's greatest vineyard, to the village wines to upgrade their reputation. The Grands Crus were similarly allowed to add Chambertin's name to their own.

The wines of Chambertin and its Grand Cru neighbours are the most long-lasting of all red Burgundies. Vosne wines are more classic, more majestic, but Gevreys are the most voluptuous.

Gevrey-Chambertin, with a fine church and château, is the only village of any real size and consequence between Nuits and Dijon and is a pleasant place in which to stroll. As well as plenty of shops, owners' wine boutiques and restaurants with meals at various prices, there are at least 40 good, reliable growers. Encouragingly, a good proportion of these domaines are run by talented young winemakers, many of whom have built up their estates from scratch.

After Gevrey continue north, through Fixin with its fine church (now deconsecrated) set among the vines, and Couchey, where Philippe Naddef makes exemplary red wines, to Marsannay, known for its delicious Pinot Noir rosé. Unusually for the Côte de Nuits, there is some white wine too. Small amounts of white also come from Fixin, Morey and Nuits-St-Georges. In Marsannay it's worth stopping at Bruno Clair.

Gevrey-Chambertin's 15th-century château was orignally built by an abbot of Cluny to store his wine.

At the north end of Marsannay, as you reach the suburbs of Dijon, the vines peter out and the Côte de Nuits comes to an end. In Chenôve, the Cuverie des Ducs de Bourgogne contains two magnificent medieval presses capable of filling 100 casks in a single pressing. They are still used occasionally. In the rue Jules Blaizet there are some 13th-century vineyard labourers' cottages.

From Chenôve it is a short distance either to Dijon, the historic capital of Burgundy, or to the main N74 road that leads back to Nuits-St-Georges. Having passed through the tiny village of Vougeot (where you can visit grower Alain Hudelot-Noëllat), make a final stop at the lower end of Clos de Vougeot in front of the many pretentious gateways advertising the owners' names. Remember, however, that the best Vougeot comes from the other end of the vineyard toward the top of the slope, on the same contour level as the Côte de Nuits' other Grands Crus. After Vougeot it is a short detour off the N74 to visit Emmanuel Rouget in the village of Flagey-Échézeaux before returning to Nuits.

Côte de Nuits Fact File

Dijon, a large bustling city with many fine restaurants, and the wine town of Nuits-St-Georges are the main centres. Dijon's tourist offices can provide information for the whole of the Côte d'Or.

Information

Both the BIVB and the Syndicat d'Initiative have lists of growers to visit and can set up appointments. Ask also for the brochure listing Portes Ouvertes.

BIVB
12 boulevard Bretonnière, 21204 Beaune. Tel 03 80 25 04 80; fax 03 80 25 04 81.
Wine information, maps, lists of cellars to visit and wine courses in the Côte d'Or.

Comité Régional du Tourisme
34 rue des Forges, 21000 Dijon. Tel 03 80 44 11 44; fax 03 80 30 90 02.

Gîtes de France
27 rue Auguste Comte, 21000 Dijon. Tel 03 80 72 06 05; fax 03 80 73 25 60.
Simple accommodation for those who enjoy self-catering.

Syndicat d'Initiative
Rue Sonays, 21700 Nuits-St-Georges. Tel 03 80 61 22 47; fax 03 80 61 30 98.

La Confrérie des Chevaliers du Tastevin
Founded during the 1930s Depression, the Confrérie exists to promote local wines. It owns the Château du Clos de Vougeot, where periodic investitures to join the 'club' and great banquets are held amid great razzmatazz. These are not open to the public, though local merchants can invite some of their better customers, or customers' customers to the dinners.

Growers can also submit bottles to the Confrérie for tasting approval and those wines that pass are allowed to use a special 'Tastevinage' label.

Château du Clos de Vougeot
21640 Vougeot. Tel 03 80 62 86 09; fax 03 80 62 82 75.

This medieval château was owned by the monks of Cîteaux until the French Revolution. Restored in the 19th century, it is the Côte de Nuits' most famous landmark. Surrounded by vines within the walled Clos de Vougeot Grand Cru, the château has a grand cellar dating from the 12th century, where

the banquets take place, and there are other vestiges of its monastic past.

Cuverie des Ducs de Bourgogne
21200 Chenôve. Tel 03 80 52 51 30 (ask for the *service culturel*). Contains two huge medieval wine presses and other artefacts connected with wine-making.

Where to Buy Wine

Most growers offer wines for sale and will let you taste them first. Look for the sign Dégustation Vente in the wine villages.

Caveau de Bacchus
19 rue Crébillon, 21700 Nuits-St-Georges. Tel 03 80 61 15 32. This shop has an interesting choice of local wines.

Maison des Hautes-Côtes
See p.30.

Château de Marsannay
21160 Marsannay-la-Côte. Tel 03 80 51 71 11; fax 03 80 51 71 12.
Owned by the Beaune firm of Patriarche, this tastefully restored château has a medieval cellar and small wine museum. A wine tour, a *tastevin* and tasting of 12 wines are also on offer.

Markets

Dijon – daily, in the Halles Centrales
Nuits-St-Georges – Friday morning

The small town of Nuits-St-Georges is the commercial centre of the region.

Festivals and Events

Dijon's wine festival takes place at the end of August, but better known is the city's 2-week International Gastronomic Fair in early November.

As with the more famous Hospices de Beaune (see p.37), vineyards in the Côte de Nuits, mainly from the Nuits-St-Georges AC, have been donated over the years to the local Hospices. The Hospices de Nuits wines are auctioned every year on the Sunday preceding Palm Sunday. There is also a wine fair.

Each January, the festival of St-Vincent Tournante, the patron saint of *vignerons*, is held in a different village along the Côte d'Or. The growers of that particular village also hold open-house throughout the weekend. Many of the wine villages also celebrate the end of the vintage.

Where to Stay and Eat

Le Chambolle-Musigny Ⓡ
Rue Basse, 21220 Chambolle-Musigny. Tel 03 89 62 86 26. Ⓕ
Friendly, simple restaurant with good wine list, especially of local wines. Park outside the Post Office further up the hill.

Hostellerie Chapeau Rouge Ⓗ Ⓡ
5 rue Michelet, 21000 Dijon. Tel 03 80 30 28 10; fax 03 80 30 33 89. Ⓕ Ⓕ Ⓕ
The best hotel in Dijon, centrally located, with a very good restaurant and excellent wine list.

Le Clos du Roy Ⓡ
35 avenue du 14 juillet, 21300 Chenôve. Tel & fax 03 80 51 33 66. Ⓕ Ⓕ
Stylish cooking and a warm welcome from the Poillot family can be expected here.

L'Écuyer de Bourgogne Ⓡ
21160 Couchey. Tel 03 80 52 03 14. Ⓕ
Good value at this little bistro in rather self-conscious rustic surroundings. It makes a good place to stop for lunch in the northern Côte de Nuits.

Château de Gilly Ⓗ Ⓡ
21640 Gilly-lès-Cîteaux. Tel 03 80 62 89 98; fax 03 80 62 82 34. Ⓕ Ⓕ Ⓕ
This moated, former Cistercian abbey is near Clos de Vougeot. *Relais et Châteaux.* Good but expensive food and wine.

Hostellerie La Gentilhommière Ⓗ Ⓡ
Route Meuilley, 21700 Nuits-St-Georges. Tel 03 80 61 12 06; fax 03 80 61 30 33. Ⓕ Ⓕ
A restful place to stay, set outside the main conurbation alongside the river Meuzin. Reasonable restaurant. Swimming pool.

Gourmets Ⓡ
8 rue Puits de Têt, 21160 Marsannay. Tel 03 80 52 16 32; fax 03 80 52 03 01. Ⓕ Ⓕ
Round the corner from the church, M. Perreault serves classy food in relatively simple surroundings. Good wine list.

Hôtel Les Grands Crus Ⓗ
21200 Gevrey-Chambertin. Tel 03 80 34 34 15; fax 03 80 51 89 07. Ⓕ Ⓕ
Peaceful, modern hotel on the edge of Gevrey. Stylish rooms.

Bistrot des Halles Ⓡ
10 rue Bannelier, 21000 Dijon. Tel 03 80 49 94 15. Ⓕ
Simple bistro in the same street as some excellent cheese shops.

The Hostellerie Chapeau Rouge is located in the heart of Dijon near the medieval Palais des Ducs.

Maison des Hautes-Côtes Ⓡ
21700 Marey-lès-Fussey. Tel 03 80 62 91 29. Ⓕ
Lively, crowded restaurant serving traditional Burgundian food but of only average quality. Various local producers have their wines on show here and you can taste them upstairs before eating. Information on what to do and see in the Hautes-Côtes is also available.

Robert Losset Ⓡ
Place de l'Église, 21640 Flagey-Échézeaux. Tel 03 80 62 88 10. Ⓕ
Good-value regional food, and lots of it, served without frills. Short variable wine list.

Hôtel le Manassès Ⓗ
21200 Curtil-Vergy. Tel 03 80 61 43 81; fax 03 80 61 42 79. Ⓕ Ⓕ
Up in the Hautes-Côtes, this hotel is small, quiet and secluded, but the owner, Yves Chaley, can be voluble. He has his own (good) vineyard (the Domaine du Val de Vergy) as well as a small wine-making museum.

Les Millésimes Ⓡ
25 rue l'Église, 21220 Gevrey-Chambertin. Tel 03 80 51 84 24; fax 03 80 34 12 73. Ⓕ Ⓕ Ⓕ
The best, but by far the most expensive, place to eat in Gevrey. Elegant surroundings. Very good food and lengthy, but expensive, wine list.

L'Orée du Bois Ⓡ
21220 Quemigny-Poisot. Tel & fax 03 80 49 78 77. Ⓕ
This little modern auberge-style restaurant, up in the hills above Gevrey-Chambertin, provides stylish variations on local dishes. Good wine list.

Le Petit Caveau Ⓡ
4 Rue Richebourg, 21220 Gevrey-Chambertin. Tel 03 89 34 32 83. Ⓕ
In the middle of the village, this husband-and-wife team offers good-value, simple food and friendly service. Good wine list.

Le Pré aux Clercs Ⓡ
13 Place de la Libération, 21000 Dijon. Tel 03 80 38 05 05; fax 03 80 38 16 16. Ⓕ Ⓕ Ⓕ
Opposite the Palais des Ducs this restaurant serves high-quality cooking in unpretentious surroundings. Good wine list.

Thibert Ⓡ
10 Place Wilson, 21000 Dijon. Tel 03 80 67 74 64; fax 03 80 63 87 72. Ⓕ Ⓕ Ⓕ
The best restaurant, not just in Dijon, but for a considerable area around. The Hotel Wilson is next door. Fine wine list.

Hôtel Wilson Ⓗ
Place Wilson, 21000 Dijon. Tel 03 80 66 82 50; fax 03 80 36 41 54. Ⓕ Ⓕ
A charming old coaching inn. Near enough to the local sights. Eat at Thibert next door.

Château André Ziltener Ⓗ
21220 Chambolle-Musigny. Tel 03 80 62 41 62; fax 03 80 62 83 75. Ⓕ Ⓕ Ⓕ
A fine 18th-century country house. Very definitely de luxe throughout, with prices to match. Tastings of the domaine's own wines.

Wines and Wine Villages

The Côte de Nuits produces almost entirely red wine and these wines can be some of the firmest and longest lasting of all Burgundies. The Route des Grands Crus links the wine villages, which are mainly set away from the busy N74 road that joins Dijon and Nuits-St-Georges.

Brochon Minor wine village squeezed in between Gevrey-Chambertin and Fixin. The better wines are sold as Gevrey-Chambertin, the less good ones as Côte de Nuits-Villages.

Chambolle-Musigny AC
Chambolle lies nestling in the hills with its vineyards below. There are some interesting wall paintings in the fine 16th-century church. The village produces delicious soft, fragrant, raspberry-flavoured red wines, the best of which have real intensity and elegance.
Chambolle has two great Grands Crus, Musigny and Bonnes-Mares, which could not be more different. Musigny is the epitome of delicacy, harmony, complexity and finesse and is often the finest wine in Burgundy. Bonnes-Mares is denser, more solid and slower to develop, and the richness of the fruit arrives only after several years. There are 24 Premiers Crus, the best known of which are les Amoureuses, les Charmes, les Cras and les Fuées.
Best producers: Amiot-Servelle, GHISLAINE BARTHOD, *Pierre Berthaut, J Frédéric Mugnier at Ch. de Chambolle-Musigny,* GEORGES ROUMIER, COMTE GEORGES DE VOGÜE.

Chenôve The most northerly commune in the Côte de Nuits is more a suburb of Dijon than a wine village. Vineyards in the southern part of Chenôve use the Marsannay AC and the rest the Bourgogne AC. The Cuveries des Ducs de Bourgogne is worth visiting.

Comblanchien This village at the southern end of the Côte de Nuits is as important for marble as for wine. The wines are sold as Côte de Nuits-Villages.

Corgoloin This is the southernmost village in the Côte de Nuits and, like Comblanchien, is also a quarrying centre. The wines are Côte de Nuits-Villages.

Côte de Nuits-Villages AC
This is a useful AC for mainly red wine from either end of the Côte, from Brochon and Fixin in the north, and Prémeaux-Prissey, Comblanchien and Corgoloin in the south.
The wines are fuller and richer than straight red Burgundy, but too robust and unrefined to be proper village wines in their own right.
Best producers: DENIS BACHELET *(Gevrey-Chambertin),* DANIEL RION ET FILS *(Nuits-St-Georges).*

The D122 road, better known as the Route des Grands Crus, winds its way between the wine villages.

Couchey The vineyards of this small village are included in the Marsannay AC.

Fixin AC The northernmost quality wine village in the Côte de Nuits, Fixin produces mainly red wines that are full, rich and robust, a little hard at first and slow to develop. The lesser wines may be sold as Côte de Nuits-Villages. Fixin is also one of the few villages in the Côte de Nuits to produce any white

wine. There are 6 Premiers Crus, which lie at the top end of the village on a fairly steep slope.
Best producers: Pierre Gelin.

Flagey-Échézeaux East of the N74 and the railway line, right off the beaten track, the sleepy village of Flagey stands isolated from its vincyards, which lie in a pocket of land up the slope from Vosne and Vougeot. Its village wines are sold as Vosne-Romanée, leaving merely the Grands Crus of Échézeaux and Grands-Échézeaux. Échézeaux is an inexpensive Grand Cru and the wine can vary in quality. It always has a certain robustness, a slight lack of the breeding found in more illustrious wines. Grands-Échézeaux is distinctly better, both more concentrated and classier.
Best producers: EMMANUEL ROUGET.

Gevrey-Chambertin AC
This is one of the largest and most important wine villages in Burgundy. The village AC land overflows onto the eastern, flatter side of the N74, as does the village itself. Always red, a Gevrey wine is full, rich and concentrated, with a hint of chocolate/coffee/caramel spice. The more northern slopes add a touch of robustness to the wine, but less elegance.
There are 9 Grands Crus stretching south of the village to the border with Morey-St-Denis. Chambertin and Chambertin-Clos de Bèze are several steps above the others in quality and compete with the best ones in Vosne-Romanée for the title of greatest red *climat* in Burgundy. Here Pinot Noir makes big, strong and intense wines that need 10–15 years to mellow to a perfumed, plummy richness.
Latricières-Chambertin, adjacent to Chambertin on the Morey side, exhibits a touch of spice and robustness. Mazis-Chambertin and Ruchottes-Chambertin, at the northern end

of this line of Grands Crus and nearest to the village itself, are more refined but can be a little less intense.

The D122 road traverses the Grands Crus from north to south and the Grands Crus below it are not quite in the same league. Mazoyères-Chambertin and Charmes-Chambertin are soft, plump and enjoyable, without quite the depth of the top rank. Most Mazoyères growers sell their wine as Charmes-Chambertin. Griottes-Chambertin can be exquisitely fruity but round rather than with real depth. Chapelle-Chambertin is somewhat lacking in definition.

There are 26 Premiers Crus, including Clos-St-Jacques, les Cazetières, Lavaut-St-Jacques, les Estournelles, la Combe aux Moines and les Combottes. There is a large number of good growers in Gevrey, some of whom produce a Vieilles Vignes village wine that can be very good value.

Best producers: DENIS BACHELET, *Lucien Boillot et Fils,* ALAIN BURGUET, *Philippe Charlopin-Parizot, Philippe Damoy,* CLAUDE DUGAT, BERNARD DUGAT-PY, ANDRÉ ET FRÉDÉRIC ESMONIN, MICHEL ESMONIN ET FILLE, *Vincent Geantet-Pansiot, Bernard Maume,* DENIS MORTET, JOSEPH ROTY, ARMAND ROUSSEAU, CHRISTIAN SERAFIN.

Grands Crus Burgundy's 32 Grands Crus represent the very best soils and locations and, therefore in principle, the best wine that the region is capable of producing. Most of the Grands Crus are split up between a number of different growers – Clos de Vougeot is divided between more than 80 owners – and, not surprisingly, the quality can vary. In the Côte de Nuits there are 24 Grands Crus, all for red wine. They account for about 10 per cent of all Côte de Nuits wine. The Grands Crus are listed below by village. For further descriptions, see the village entries in this section.

Chambolle-Musigny
Musigny (10.9ha),
Bonnes-Mares (15.1ha).

Flagey-Échézeaux
Échézeaux (37.7ha),
Grands-Échézeaux (9.1ha).
Gevrey-Chambertin
Chambertin (12.9ha),
Chambertin-Clos-de-Bèze
(15.4ha), Latricières-Chambertin
(7.4ha), Mazis-Chambertin
(9.1ha), Ruchottes-Chambertin
(3.3ha), Charmes-Chambertin
and Mazoyères-Chambertin
(30.8ha), Griottes-Chambertin
(2.7ha), Chapelle-Chambertin
(5.5ha).

Arcenant is one of several pretty wine villages in the Hautes-Côtes de Nuits.

Morey-St-Denis
Clos de Tart (7.5ha),
Clos des Lambrays (8.8ha),
Clos St-Denis (6.6ha),
Clos de la Roche (16.9ha).
Vosne-Romanée
Romanée-Conti (1.8ha),
la Tâche (6.1ha), la Romanée
(0.9ha), Richebourg (8.0ha),
Romanée-St-Vivant (9.4ha),
Grande Rue (1.7ha).
Vougeot
Clos de Vougeot (50.6ha).

Hautes-Côtes de Nuits AC
Up in the hills, behind the Côte d'Or, the soil is the same limestone that produces the great Burgundies below, but the climate is colder and the vineyards can, therefore, be more exposed. Nevertheless, the last 30 years have seen a huge expansion of vineyards here, and the results, especially in hot summers, are encouraging for both red and white wine. The main wine villages are Arcenant,

Bévy, Chavannes, Collonges-lès-Bevy, Concoeur-et-Corboin, Curtil-Vergy, Magny-lès-Villers, Marey-lès-Fussey, Messanges, Meuilley, Villers-la-Faye and Villars-Fontaine.
Best producers: Yves Chaley (Curtil-Vergy), Patrick Hudelot (Villars-Fontaine), ROBERT JAYER-GILLES *(Magny-lès-Villers).*

Marsannay AC Long famous for its delicious Pinot Noir rosé, which was sold as AC Bourgogne until 1987, Marsannay is now a village AC in its own right for red, white and rosé. Vineyards in Chenôve and Couchey can also use the AC. Medium-bodied, the red is for early drinking. Unusually for the Côte de Nuits, there is also a little white.
Best producers: BRUNO CLAIR.

Morey-St-Denis AC Morey has an imposing church and some fine bourgeois residences, but its wine has always led a schizophrenic existence, being on the one hand neither as soft and fragrant as Chambolle, its southern neighbour, nor on the other as full and vigorous as Gevrey, its northern neighbour. But its lack of identity helps to keep prices relatively low. There are 4 Grands Crus – Clos de Tart and Clos des Lambrays are in sole ownership of the Mommessin and the Saier family respectively. Clos de Tart seems to follow the style of its Chambolle neighbour, Bonnes-Mares, while Clos des Lambrays produces lighter wine as a result of having more sand in the soil. Clos St-Denis is equally more delicate, more red-fruit flavoured than the richer, more succulent, cassis-flavoured Clos de la Roche. All 4 Grands Crus produce fine wines, but they are not as good as either of Chambolle's Grands Crus or the best in Gevrey.

There are 20 Premiers Crus, most of which are very small. The best known is Clos des Ormes. A little white wine comes from the slopes above Clos de la Roche.

Best producers: DUJAC, ROBERT GROFFIER, *Domaine des Lambrays, Hubert Lignier, Mommessin, Perrot-Minot, Ponsot.*

Nuits-St-Georges AC Nuits-St-Georges is the commercial centre of the northern Côte d'Or, but, as the N74 goes straight through the town, it has little of Beaune's medieval charm. Several of the main shopping streets in the centre of Nuits have been pedestrianized. The late Romanesque church of St-Symphonien is worth a visit.

The vineyards lie in two groups, north and south of the town. The AC also covers vineyards in Prémeaux-Prissey. Here in the Clos de l'Arlot vineyard the Côte d'Or is at its narrowest – from the top of the slope to the bottom of the AC vineyards the distance measures a mere 300m (1000ft), while only a short distance away in the Côte de Beaune at Savigny and Chorey-lès-Beaune the vineyards stretch east to west for as much as 5km (3 miles).

Nuits' wine is rich, full and muscular and nearly always has a certain robustness. There are no Grand Cru vineyards, but to compensate there are 41 Premiers Crus. The best are Boudots on the Vosne boundary, les St-Georges, les Vaucrains, les Cailles and les Porrets-St-Georges. A few growers produce white wine, either Gouges from mutated Pinot Noir vines or

from Chardonnay or a blend of the two.

Best producers: *Arlot, Jean Chauvenet, Robert Chevillon, Jean-Jacques Confuron,* FAIVELEY, HENRI GOUGES, *Moillard-Grivot/Thomas Moillard,* DANIEL RION.

Premiers Crus Below the category of Grands Crus come the Premiers Crus, of which there are some 139 in the Côte de Nuits. The Nuits-St-Georges AC has the most, with 26. Like the Grands Crus, these vineyards are ideally situated in the middle of the slope, where aspect, drainage and protection from the prevailing winds are at their optimum. Similarly, nearly all of them are in multi-ownership. One or two Premiers Crus – Clos-St-Jacques in Gevrey, les Amoreuses in Chambolle, les St-Georges in Nuits, for instance, can produce wine every bit as good as most Grands Crus.

Many of the Côte de Nuits' top vineyards are easily identifiable by stone markers such as this one.

Vosne-Romanée AC
Though a sizeable village, Vosne has no great architecture, having been largely destroyed in the Franco-Prussian war of 1870–71. Nor is there much life: just a simple village shop and small post office. You get the feeling that everyone is either out in the vineyards or busy in their cellars. Wine is their calling, and a serious one. And, of course, the wine, red only, is very seriously good too: full, a little austere in its youth, very majestic and pure in flavour, very intense and

concentrated and very long and complex on the palate. Burgundy reaches for perfection here.

Of the 6 Grands Crus, 4 are in sole ownership: the Domaine de la Romanée-Conti owns Romanée-Conti and la Tâche, the Liger-Belair family owns la Romanée (the smallest AC in France) and the Lamarche family owns Grande Rue. Romanée-Conti is wine at its apogee of refinement, harmony and pure fruit. La Tâche can be richer and fuller bodied – and sometimes as good. La Romanée, further up the slope, is a little leaner. Richebourg is lush, abundant, voluptuous and seductive. Romanée-St-Vivant, fragrant, elegant, feminine, is the closest in style to Musigny. Sadly, Grande Rue is a continual disappointment.

There are 16 Premiers Crus, the best-known of which are les Beaux-Monts, les Brulées, les Malconsorts and les Suchots.

Best producers: ROBERT ARNOUX, *Cathiard,* BRUNO CLAVELIER, CONFURON-COTÉTIDOT, RENÉ ENGEL, RÉGIS FOREY, JEAN GRIVOT, ANNE ET FRANÇOIS GROS, *Gros Frère et Soeur,* JEAN ET MICHEL GROS, *Alfred Hagelen-Jayer,* LEROY, MÉO-CAMUZET, *Jean Mongeard-Mugneret,* MUGNERET-GIBOURG/DR GEORGES MUGNERET, DOMAINE DE LA ROMANÉE-CONTI, *Jean Tardy.*

Vougeot AC The small village of Vougeot lies on the main N74 road just beyond the foot of the famous Clos de Vougeot, Burgundy's largest Grand Cru. Not surprisingly, this Grand Cru varies considerably. The wine from the top of the slope can be very fine: medium-full and succulent, with a touch of spice, but critics argue that soil at the bottom of the vineyard is hardly even of Premier Cru level.

Clos de Vougeot forms the bulk of Vougeot's wines, but there are also 4 Premiers Crus and a few vineyards using the village name. You are better off sticking to wine from Chambolle or Vosne.

Best producers: *Bertagna, Ch. de la Tour,* ALAIN HUDELOT-NOËLLAT.

Half-way up the hill near the border between the villages of Puligny-Montrachet and Chassagne-Montrachet, these are some of the most valuable white wine vineyards in the world. Below the path is the Montrachet Grand Cru and above it, on the right, is the steeper, rockier Chevalier-Montrachet Grand Cru, the top two of five white wine Grands Crus in the immediate locality. These Grands Crus benefit from a perfect altitude (between 260 and 290m/850 and 950ft), ideal south-facing exposure, good drainage on a gradual slope, and precisely the right mixture of various limestones and other soil elements – all these factors combine to produce the most profound, long-lasting Chardonnays in all Burgundy.

Beaune

Dijon may be Burgundy's administrative capital, but Beaune is its wine heart. Surrounded and protected by its *périphérique* road and old ramparts, the ancient centre, with its dense maze of narrow streets full of tall, medieval buildings, is still largely unspoiled. The streets are increasingly pedestrianized, and there are countless shops in which to buy everything to do with wine as well as wonderful food for picnics out in the wine villages.

The best way to discover Beaune is to stroll around the town. Place Carnot is the focal point and only a couple of minutes' walk away lie the decorative Hôtel-Dieu, the centre of the Hospices de Beaune, and the excellent wine museum housed in the medieval Hôtel des Ducs de Bourgogne. Wander freely: there are delightful hidden alleyways, cobbled streets, private courtyards and medieval buildings. Within the thick walls that surround the town, under your feet even, in the honeycombed old cellars, millions of bottles of Burgundy lie quietly asleep in cellars, awaiting their maturity.

The flamboyant 15th-century Gothic Hôtel-Dieu is headquarters to the Hospices de Beaune, a charitable foundation famous for its November wine auction.

The Hospices de Beaune

The Hospices de Beaune consists of two charitable institutions, the Hôtel-Dieu founded in 1443 by Nicolas de Rolin, chancellor under Philip the Good, and his wife, after an outbreak of plague in Beaune, and the 17th-century Hospice de la Charité. Built to house the sick and poor, the Hôtel-Dieu with its famous painting, *The Last Judgment* by Van der Weyden, is Beaune's most famous landmark by a long way. Over the years, the Hospices have received donations of valuable vineyard land and these now total almost 60ha, most of them Premiers Crus, mainly located in the Côte de Beaune. On the third Sunday of November these vineyard yields (most of the wines are named after their original benefactor) are sold at a grand charity auction that is attended by buyers from all round the world. The prices paid for the month-old wines reflect the quality of the new vintage and the current economic mood.

This auction is the central event of the weekend of *les Trois Glorieuses*. There are also three magnificent feasts: in the Château du Clos de Vougeot, in a cellar in the walls (*bastions*) of Beaune (these are both evening affairs) and the lunchtime Paulée de Meursault. During this weekend Beaune is crammed to bursting. Not only is every merchant's and grower's cellar door open, and the Hospices wines available for tasting, but there is a huge fair of all Burgundy's wines in the Palais des Congrès. For three days Beaune is *en fête*, before relapsing into its usual winter somnolence.

Beaune Fact File

At the intersection of two busy motorways and with many hotels, restaurants and wine shops, Beaune makes an obvious stopping point for any visitor to Burgundy.

Information

Office du Tourisme
Rue de l'Hôtel-Dieu, 21200 Beaune. Tel 03 80 26 21 30; fax 03 80 26 21 39. Information on Chambres d'Hôtes and Portes Ouvertes as well as town maps of Beaune and other useful leaflets.

BIVB
12 boulevard Bretonnière, 21204 Beaune. Tel 03 80 25 04 80; fax 03 80 25 04 81. Wine information, maps and lists of Côte d'Or growers to visit.

Hôtel-Dieu
Rue de l'Hôtel-Dieu, 21200 Beaune. Tel 03 80 24 45 00; fax 03 80 24 45 99. Beaune's most famous building, with its magnificent architecture, is now a fine museum with works of art. There is a *Son et Lumière* on summer evenings.

Musée du Vin de Bourgogne
Hôtel des Ducs de Bourgogne, rue d'Enfer, 21200 Beaune. Tel 03 80 22 08 19; fax 03 80 24 56 20. Interesting wine museum and works of art displayed in the former residence of the dukes of Burgundy.

Athenaeum de la Vigne et du Vin
7 rue de l'Hôtel-Dieu, 21200 Beaune. Tel 03 80 25 08 30; fax 03 80 25 08 31. Huge selection of wine and food books, as well as exhibitions.

Markets

Saturday morning in the Place Carnot and surrounding streets.

Where to Buy Wine

Beaune has a multitude of wine shops and wine cellars, all inviting the tourist to taste and buy. However, not all of these can be recommended. Often it is the worst wines that are the most easily available.

Patriarche Père et Fils
Marché aux Vins, rue Nicolas Rolin, 21200 Beaune. Tel 03 80 22 27 69; fax 03 80 22 75 72. An interesting visit to the largest cellars in Burgundy.

Perardel
Avenue Charles de Gaulle, 21200 Beaune. Tel 03 80 24 08 09; fax 03 80 24 79 00. Good selection of French wines.

Denis Perret
Place Carnot, 21200 Beaune. Tel 03 80 22 35 47; fax 03 80 22 57 33. A wide range of wines from 5 merchants: Bouchard Père et Fils, Chanson, Drouhin, Jadot and Latour.

Beaune's weekly market and fine food shops are a good source of picnic fare to enjoy out in the vineyards.

La Reine Pédauque
2 faubourg St-Nicolas, 21200 Beaune. Tel 03 80 22 23 11; fax 03 80 22 70 23. Free tasting of 3 wines follows a tour of this merchant's extensive cellars.

Festivals and Events

The November Hospices de Beaune wine auction is the main event of *Les Trois Glorieuses* (see p.36) when wine lovers visit the town from all over the world.

Where to Stay and Eat

Le Cep Ⓗ
27 rue Maufoux, 21200 Beaune. Tel 03 80 22 35 48; fax 03 80 22 76 80. Ⓕ Ⓕ Ⓕ
Close to the Hôtel-Dieu. Old-fashioned and comfortable. Eat at Bernard Morillon next door.

La Closerie Ⓗ
61 route de Pommard, 21200 Beaune. Tel 03 80 22 15 07; fax 03 80 24 16 22. Ⓕ Ⓕ
Comfortable modern hotel on the edge of town with a swimming pool.

L'Ecusson Ⓡ
Place Malmédy, 21200 Beaune. Tel 03 80 24 03 82; fax 03 80 24 74 02. Ⓕ Ⓕ
Small restaurant with imaginative cooking and eclectic wine list.

Le Gourmandin Ⓡ
8 place Carnot, 21200 Beaune. Tel 03 80 24 07 88; fax 03 80 22 27 42. Ⓕ
Relaxed service and good, simple food. Imaginative wine list.

Henri II Ⓗ
12 faubourg St-Nicolas, 21200 Beaune. Tel 03 80 22 83 84; fax 03 80 24 15 13. Ⓕ Ⓕ
On the main exit north by the *périphérique*, but not as noisy as this might seem. Most rooms are in a modern annexe at the back.

Jardin des Remparts Ⓡ
10 rue Hôtel-Dieu, 21200 Beaune. Tel 03 80 24 79 41; fax 03 80 24 92 79. Ⓕ Ⓕ
Airy dining-room with tables in the garden in summer. Stylish food and good wine list.

Maxime Ⓡ
3 place Madeleine, 21200 Beaune. Tel 03 80 22 17 82; fax 03 80 24 90 81. Ⓕ
Good bistro and excellent value.

Bernard Morillon Ⓡ
31 rue Maufoux, 21200 Beaune. Tel 03 80 24 12 06; fax 03 80 22 66 22. Ⓕ Ⓕ
Next to Le Cep. Very competent, if old-fashioned, cuisine. Good wine list.

The Corton Grand Cru, rising steeply above the village of Aloxe-Corton, is well protected by the wooded ridge on top of the hill. The vineyards producing straight Aloxe-Corton are in the foreground.

Map illustrations: (above) Wayside cross among the vineyards; (centre) the medieval cellars at Ch. de Meursault; (below) many gateways to specific plots of vines in the Côte d'Or are inscribed with the names of the owner and also the vineyard.

TOUR SUMMARY

The tour starts in Beaune, the wine capital of Burgundy, and visits wine villages along the Côte and up in the scenic Hautes-Côtes.

Distance covered 80km (50 miles)

Time needed 3½ hours, excluding detours.

Terrain The journey comprises main roads and *départementale* routes that are easy to negotiate.

Hotels Beaune offers the biggest range of accommodation, but there are good hotels in the surrounding villages as well.

Restaurants There are plenty of fine restaurants in and around Beaune, but the options in the surrounding countryside are more limited.

Côte de Beaune

The Côte de Beaune is more varied in character than the Côte de Nuits – it is longer, wider, more gently inclined and more south-facing. Although Côte de Beaune vineyards actually produce more red wine than white, it is here, in the world-famous villages of Meursault, Puligny and Chassagne, and on part of the Corton hill, that the Chardonnay grape comes into its own.

The Côte de Beaune begins in the north with a flourish at the Corton hill, which overlooks the villages of Ladoix, Aloxe and Pernand on three sides and continues south past the red wine villages of Savigny, Beaune, Pommard and Volnay before dividing. The main slope then continues through Meursault on to Santenay and Maranges, while another hillside leads up to Monthélie, Auxey-Duresses and St-Romain before disappearing into the Hautes-Côtes.

The wines of the Côte de Beaune are more varied than those of the Côte de Nuits. Corton is the only red Grand Cru, but high-quality reds can also be found in Pommard and Volnay. At the other end of the scale, wine from the lesser villages and cooler slopes can be blended together under the catch-all appellation of Côte de Beaune-Villages, a useful and inexpensive introduction to red Burgundy. There is no equivalent white blend, but the wines of Savigny and Pernand to the north – Auxey-Duresses, St-Romain, St-Aubin and Santenay – can each fill this role, while at the top of the scale Corton-Charlemagne and the four white Grands Crus adjoining the Montrachet Grand Cru show that Chardonnay can be at its greatest in Burgundy as well as Pinot Noir.

The Tour

Leave Beaune, heading north to Savigny-lès-Beaune ('lès' indicating close to) on the D18 and D2. The *autoroute* marks the boundary between Beaune and Savigny. The Savigny vineyards are divided in two by the valley of the Rhoin river which bubbles out of the Hautes-Côtes. The Premiers Crus of Marconnets, Peuillets, Jarrons and Narbantons face almost north, while on the opposite flank, below the Bois Noël, Serpentières, Guettes, Lavières and, best of all, Vergelesses, face south. Savigny, a modest little village but with an imposing castle, has plenty of good growers, such as Simon Bize and Chandon de Briailles, and the wines, if sometimes a little rough and ready, are cheaper than those of Beaune, so are good value.

For an optional detour (allow 30 minutes for the journey, plus stopping time) continue on the D2 beyond Savigny toward Bouilland. The road leads along a very

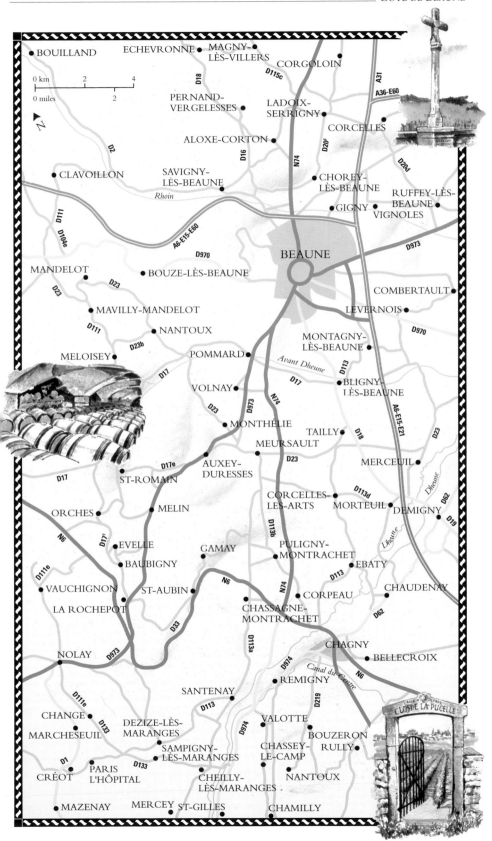

BOUILLAND
ECHEVRONNE
MAGNY-LÈS-VILLERS
CORGOLOIN
D115c
D18
A31
A36-E60
0 km 2 4
0 miles 2
N
PERNAND-VERGELESSES
LADOIX-SERRIGNY
CORCELLES
D2
ALOXE-CORTON
D16
N74
D20f
D20d
CLAVOILLON
SAVIGNY-LÈS-BEAUNE
Rhoin
CHOREY-LÈS-BEAUNE
RUFFEY-LÈS-BEAUNE
VIGNOLES
GIGNY
D11q
D10de
A6-E15-E60
D970
BEAUNE
D973
MANDELOT
BOUZE-LÈS-BEAUNE
COMBERTAULT
D23
D23
MAVILLY-MANDELOT
LEVERNOIS
D111
NANTOUX
D970
D23b
MONTAGNY-LÈS-BEAUNE
MELOISEY
POMMARD
Avant Dheune
D113
D17
BLIGNY-LÈS-BEAUNE
VOLNAY
D973
N74
D17
A6-E15-E21
D23
D23
MONTHÉLIE
TAILLY
D18
MEURSAULT
D17e
AUXEY-DURESSES
D23
MERCEUIL
D17
ST-ROMAIN
Dheune
D113d
D62
ORCHES
MELIN
CORCELLES-LES-ARTS
MORTEUIL
DEMIGNY
D19
D113b
N6
D17'
EVELLE
GAMAY
PULIGNY-MONTRACHET
Uhaine
D111e
BAUBIGNY
EBATY
D113
CHAUDENAY
VAUCHIGNON
ST-AUBIN
N6
N74
CORPEAU
LA ROCHEPOT
D33
CHASSAGNE-MONTRACHET
D62
D113a
CHAGNY
NOLAY
D973
BELLECROIX
Canal du Centre
D974
N6
REMIGNY
SANTENAY
D113
D219
D111e
CHANGE
D138
DEZIZE-LÈS-MARANGES
D974
VALOTTE
BOUZERON
MARCHESEUIL
SAMPIGNY-LÈS-MARANGES
CHASSEY-LE-CAMP
RULLY
D1
PARIS L'HÔPITAL
D133
NANTOUX
CRÉOT
CHEILLY-LÈS-MARANGES
MAZENAY
MERCEY ST-GILLES
CHAMILLY

CLOSDE LA PUCELLE

pretty valley to the ruins of the Abbaye Ste Marguerite up in the hills. To reach it, turn left after 9km (5½ miles) through the hamlet of le Forge and follow the signs.

To continue on the main tour, leave Savigny on the D1b for Pernand-Vergelesses. As the road passes under the Bois Noël and rejoins the D18, Savigny's les Vergelesses Premier Cru becomes the Île des Vergelesses, Pernand's best Premier Cru, and the famous hill of Corton with its densely wooded top comes into full view. Stop here to take in the sight.

The south-west flank of the hill (the white Corton-Charlemagne Grand Cru) and its upper slopes on all three sides are planted with Chardonnay. Pinot Noir is planted above the villages of Aloxe and Ladoix on the south-east-facing side (the red Corton Grand Cru) and on the lower slopes where clay predominates.

Pernand is a pretty little village clinging to the side of a hill and it's worth driving up to the top and back again. Half-way up, just past the church by the *lavoir* (public washing pool) are the cellars of the famous Bonneau du Martray estate, producer of one of the best Corton-Charlemagnes. From Pernand there is also a fine view back across the flatter land toward Beaune.

The pretty village of Pernand-Vergelesses is tucked away in a valley behind the hill of Corton.

Then take the road that runs under the hill to Aloxe-Corton where there are a number of buildings with the characteristic Burgundian multi-coloured roofs. The finest example is Ch. Corton-André, owned by a wine firm. In the middle of the village turn left, follow a narrow gap between houses and continue through the vineyards. Above are Corton's best *climats*, Clos du Roi, Bressandes, Perrières and le Corton. In the middle of the vines is the *cuverie,* or vat house, belonging to the merchant Louis Latour.

Below the Corton Grand Cru land is a narrow band of Aloxe-Corton Premier Cru vineyards, followed by those qualifying for the village appellation. (One vineyard here, les Paulands, covers all three levels of the hierarchy.) Below, also, lies the village of Ladoix, on the northern side of which is Les Coquines, a very good restaurant for lunch.

Ladoix, Aloxe and Pernand share the Corton Grand Cru, the largest in Burgundy. The red is the firmest of all Côte de Beaunes, with an almost metallic hardness and austerity when young but maturing after ten years or so into a wine of richness and complexity. Growers such as Chandon de Briailles in Savigny and Prince de Mérode in Ladoix have fine ranges of red Corton. Very little white Corton is made. Corton-Charlemagne is also austere and steely, almost with a suggestion of Chablis when young, but with time it becomes rich, buttery and nutty. The wines of Bonneau du Martray, Louis Latour, Faiveley and Jadot are classic.

At Ladoix, turn right in the middle of the village down to the Ch. de Serrigny, the moated Renaissance home of the Prince de Mérode, the local *seigneur* who owns the wood at the top of the Corton hill and is one of Corton's best growers. At Ladoix take the minor D20f, parallel to the main N74, to Chorey-lès-Beaune to have a look at its moated castle. The owner, François Germain, makes good wine, as well as offering bed and breakfast (*chambres d'hôtes*). Tollot-Beaut is another good domaine here. Most of Chorey's vineyards lie on flat, fairly alluvial soil on the east side of the N74 and the wine is sold as Côte de Beaune-Villages.

Rejoin the N74 and drive south of Beaune on its *périphérique*. Once past a number of hotels and garages, and the cellar of the Hautes-Côtes co-operative on the left, the road divides. Take the D973 right, marked Autun, toward Pommard. Pommard's vineyards, like Savigny's, are also divided by a small river, the Avant Dheune, which flows out of the Hautes-Côtes, but the flank of the hills is not so indented. Its two best Premiers Crus lie on either side of the village, Épenots on the northern, Beaune side, largely behind a stone wall, and les Rugiens on the southern Volnay slope. After Corton, Pommards are the fullest, slowest-maturing wines of the Côte de Beaune, while either side of Pommard the wines of Beaune and Volnay are much lighter. Good domaines to visit include Comte Armand and Courcel. Many growers based in Volnay also make good Pommards.

From Pommard head west along the D17 up into the Hautes-Côtes de Beaune. There is mixed farming here and the vineyards are confined to the slopes with the best aspect. Take a short detour through Nantoux (Jean-Baptiste Joliot is a good grower here) and Meloisey and then on to St-Romain. At the piles of oak staves belonging to the *tonneliers* François Frères, take the road to the upper village, St-Romain le Haut. The ruins of the old castle make a good viewpoint. St-Romain wines will never be great, but from growers such as Alain Gras they are fruity and good value.

In the Hautes-Côtes the vines are planted further apart than on the lower slopes of the Côte de Beaune and in a different manner, so as to avoid frost damage and to catch every available ray of summer sun.

Drive down into the lower village and along the valley on the D17e. Turn right on the D973 to la Rochepot. A distant view of its multi-coloured castle lying above the village is one of the finest sights in this part of Burgundy. It is well worth visiting, as is the Romanesque church.

At la Rochepot take the D33 left up into the hills. This enchanting drive through the woods (a good place for a picnic) will bring you back to the Côte de Beaune via St-Aubin and Gamay. Both these pretty little villages are (just) by-passed by the N6, but the noise is still substantial. St-Aubin is some of the best-value wine in the Côte de Beaune. The reds are light and fragrant and the oak-aged whites can be excellent. An undeservedly large part of the appellation is Premier Cru which means that this designation is, therefore, of less significance here than elsewhere. Gilles Bouton, Marc Colin, Hubert Lamy and Larue are reliable growers.

Continue on the N6 (above you on the left is Mont Rachet) until you see a sign on the right and beyond it the village of Chassagne-Montrachet. Above the village you will notice (and maybe hear the noise of) another Burgundian quarry. Turn onto the D113a past Chassagne toward Santenay. Below the road on the left lies the abbey of Morgeots and above, on the right, the slopes of Chassagne's top Premiers Crus, les Caillerets, la Grande-Montagne, Grandes-Ruchottes, la Romanée and, finally, les Embrazées. Fifty years ago Chassagne was a red-wine village. Then the growers began planting Chardonnay on the upper slopes which were less clayey. The wine sold well, fetching twice the price of the red. Now nearly all Chassagne's Premier Cru vineyards are planted with Chardonnay, and there is much more Premier Cru white wine than village white.

There are many good growers in Chassagne, including Jean-Noël Gagnard, Jacques Gagnard-Delagrange and Ramonet. In the centre, near the church, is the Caveau Municipal, a wine shop owned by the village. One or two growers such as Bernard Morey also have their own shops.

Santenay's best vineyards, the Premiers Crus of Clos des Tavannes, la Comme, les Gravières and above it Beauregard, are on the boundary with Chassagne where the road does a double bend. The village itself is split into three: Santenay-le-Bas surrounding the place Jet d'Eau is the grandest part (stop for lunch here at le Terroir); Santenay-le-Haut, a straggly hamlet of narrow winding streets; and St-Jean, up in the hills under the Mont de Sène. The church of St-Jean at the foot of a horseshoe of cliffs is worth a visit.

At Santenay the long north–south slope of the Côte de Beaune comes to an end.

Because Santenay has its own spring (the water is high in lithium and *very* salty) by the vagaries of French law it is also entitled to have its own casino. This, and the baths themselves, are down in the valley by the Dheune river.

The wines of Santenay are mainly red, today increasingly elegant, and good value. Look for the names of Roger Belland and Vincent Girardin, both in the lower village. Pousse d'Or in Volnay and Louis Jadot, the Beaune merchant, also make good Santenay.

For a look at Maranges, the final appellation in the Côte d'Or, drive from Santenay-le-Haut around the corner to three small villages, Dezize, Sampigny and Cheilly – all with the suffix lès-Maranges. In Dezize the slope comes to a natural end and there is a good view to the south over the vineyards. Return through Santenay and Chassagne and cross over the N6 into Puligny-Montrachet.

The actual boundary between Chassagne and Puligny is not the main N6 road, even though it may seem like it, but is a little further north through the middle of the Montrachet and Bâtard-Montrachet Grands Crus. For many wine lovers these vineyards mark the most hallowed white wine

site on earth. Above Montrachet lies the Chevalier-Montrachet Grand Cru. Criots-Bâtard-Montrachet and Bienvenues-Bâtard-Montrachet are at opposite ends of Bâtard-Montrachet. These five vineyards, plus Corton-Charlemagne in the north, are the Côte de Beaune's famous white Grands Crus.

Hand-picking Domaine de la Romanée-Conti's vines in the Montrachet Grand Cru takes the best part of a day. The grapes are then taken to Vosne-Romanée for crushing and fermentation in barrel.

Follow the road down to the right into Puligny where there is a good restaurant with rooms, appropriately called le Montrachet, but not much else in the way of shops. The buildings here don't have cellars since the water table is too high. Some of the growers, for instance Leflaive, Carillon and Sauzet, are world-famous, but even so, no grower based in Puligny owned any of le Montrachet until a few years ago, when Leflaive bought enough vines to make one large barrel's-worth of wine. Montrachet's 8ha are now divided mainly between Bouchard Père et Fils, the Beaune merchants, the Marquis de Laguiche in Chassagne (whose wines are made by Drouhin of Beaune), Baron Thénard of Givry (whose wines are sold by Remoissenet of Beaune), and the Domaine de la Romanée-Conti (based in Vosne-Romanée). Lafon in Meursault owns a few Montrachet vines, and most of the rest is shared by growers in Chassagne, none of whom makes more than the odd cask or two of wine.

How do the white wines of the Côte de Beaune's top white wine villages – Meursault, Puligny and Chassagne – differ? In general, the wine of Meursault is softer, rounder and more nutty, with a hint of hot buttered toast. Puligny is steelier, more flowery and peachy, and seemingly higher in acidity. Chassagne resembles Puligny but is a bit more solid, perhaps even clumsy. In each village, if you find a good grower and choose a good vintage, you can buy wine that will live for a decade or more, becoming more complex and individual as it ages.

Return from the village of Puligny to the line of the Grands Crus and turn right. The road now runs north, and on either side are Puligny's best Premiers Crus: les Caillerets (which, strangely, in view of its proximity to Montrachet itself, was a red wine area until as recently as the 1950s) and Folatières up the slope, followed by a little copse and then Champs-Canet. The first vineyard on the lower side of the road is les Pucelles, which faces Bienvenues-Bâtard-Montrachet. Les Perrières and les Combettes are also on this side of the road. There are more Premiers Crus higher up the hill, including the aptly named Champs-Gain (reclaimed land), where the soil is almost entirely naked rock, but these are less highly regarded.

Meursault's best Premiers Crus are just across the boundary with Puligny: the minerally Perrières (another one!), the flowery Charmes and the citrus-tangy Genevrières. The spire of Meursault's church can be seen in the distance and you can follow it to the village. Meursault is a sizeable, lively place, with shops (including several growers' wine shops) and restaurants (although there are few decent ones). The following growers can all be visited by appointment: Ampeau, Coche-Dury, Javillier, Jobard, Lafon, Morey and Roulot. The Ch. de Meursault is also worth visiting.

From Meursault take the road out of the centre marked Volnay which leads to a camping site opposite the village of Monthélie. Turn right onto the D973. Down the slope from here, on the border of Meursault and Volnay, is a large Premier Cru vineyard called Santenots planted with Pinot Noir. Technically it is in Meursault, but in practice the wine is sold as Volnay-Santenots. Above this vineyard, and on both sides of the road, are Volnay's best vineyards, producing red wine lighter than Pommard but exquisitely subtle, fragrant and elegant, and with no lack of intensity: Clos de Chênes and Taillepieds are up the slope to the left and Caillerets and Champans below on the right.

At the first opportunity turn left into the village, which lies up the slope almost hidden in the hills. From here there is a good view to the east over vineyards and out across the plain toward the Jura. The standard of winemaking in Volnay is high and good domaines to visit include the Marquis d'Angerville, Michel Lafarge, Hubert de Montille and Pousse d'Or. From Volnay rejoin the main road, and journey back to Beaune.

Most of Monthélie's vineyards are planted with Pinot Noir and the best ones, including all but one of the Premiers Crus, are a continuation of the Volnay slope.

Côte de Beaune Fact File

The Côte de Beaune revolves around Beaune, Burgundy's wine capital (see p.36). Along the Côte itself, Meursault is the largest wine village.

Information

Office du Tourisme
See Beaune p.37.

BIVB
12 boulevard Bretonnière, 21204 Beaune. Tel 03 80 25 04 80; fax 03 80 25 04 81.
Wine information, maps and lists of growers to visit in the Côte d'Or and elsewhere in Burgundy.

Air Escargot
71150 Remigny. Tel 03 85 87 12 30; fax 03 85 87 08 84.
For leisurely balloon flights over the vineyards.

Markets

Meursault – Friday morning

Where to Buy Wine

Caveau Municipal
21190 Chassagne-Montrachet. Tel 03 80 21 38 13; fax 03 80 21 90 60.
Owned by the village, this shop sells a good range of Chassagnes at reasonable prices.

Les Caves des Hautes-Côtes
Route de Pommard, 21200 Beaune. Tel 03 80 24 63 12; fax 03 80 22 87 05.
This large co-operative on the main road south of Beaune sells a wide range of wines from the Hautes-Côtes and a smaller range of other Côte d'Or wines.

Château de Meursault
21190 Meursault. Tel 03 80 26 22 75; fax 03 80 26 22 76.
The 13th-century château with splendid vaulted medieval cellars is owned by Patriarche. The château is a large owner of Premier Cru vineyards but makes only one Meursault wine, which is good but very oaky.

Les Domaines de Pommard
Place de l'Europe, 21630 Pommard. Tel & fax 03 80 24 17 20.
Wine shop and tasting centre owned by local growers.

Festivals and Events

Every year the village of Meursault hosts the famous *Paulée.* This is the third and most informal of the three great banquets of *Les Trois Glorieuses* that surround the Hospices de Beaune auction in November (see p.36). The *Paulée* is a lunchtime affair, by invitation only, at the Ch. de Meursault, and local growers bring bottles of old wine to share.

The Banée de Meursault is a large dinner held in late March each year. Contact the Mairie de Meursault for further details (tel 03 80 21 22 62).

The other great local wine fair, which celebrates St Vincent, the patron saint of *vignerons,* takes place on the last weekend of January. Villages in the Côte

Drifting over the Meursault vineyards is a spectacular way of viewing the Côte de Beaune.

d'Or take it in turn to host the event, which combines wine-tastings, religious events and general feasting and drinking.

Where to Stay and Eat

Beaune has the best selection of hotels and restaurants in the area (see p.37). There are other good establishments along the Côte in the wine villages and up in the scenic Hautes-Côtes, but choose carefully.

La Bouzerotte Ⓡ
21200 Bouze-lès-Beaune. Tel & fax 03 80 26 01 37. Ⓕ
Run by a husband and wife team, this simple, friendly and popular bistro is up in the hills just outside Beaune. Good cooking and short, but well-chosen wine list.

Le Clarion Ⓗ
21420 Aloxe-Corton. Tel 03 80 26 46 70; fax 03 80 26 47 16. Ⓕ Ⓕ
Unpretentious, small and quiet hotel below the Corton hill. Spacious, well-decorated rooms.

Les Coquines Ⓡ
N74 Buisson, 21550 Ladoix-Serrigny. Tel 03 80 26 43 58; fax 03 80 26 49 59. Ⓕ Ⓕ
This elegant, airy restaurant on the northern outskirts of Ladoix makes an excellent lunch stop. Good food and a well-chosen wine list, with efficient service.

Relais de la Diligence Ⓡ
L'Hôpital de Meursault, 21190 Meursault. Tel 03 80 21 21 32; fax 03 80 21 64 69. Ⓕ
Large, somewhat impersonal restaurant where the 3 dining-rooms can seat more than 200 people. Its size means that it is often frequented by coach parties. Service is by local girls supervised by a rather churlish management. However, in its favour, there is a wide choice of reasonable food at varying prices and a better-than-expected wine list.

Les Genièvres Ⓗ
21200 Montagny-lès-Beaune. Tel 03 80 22 37 74; fax 03 80 24 23 18. Ⓕ
Quiet, modest hotel with elegant rooms just outside Beaune.

Hostellerie de Levernois Ⓗ Ⓡ
Levernois, 21200 Beaune. Tel 03 80 24 73 58; fax 03 80 22 75 00. Ⓕ Ⓕ Ⓕ
Luxurious, expensive *Relais et Châteaux* establishment in a large park across the *autoroute* from Beaune. Excellent restaurant and fine but expensive wine list.

Les Magnolias Ⓗ
8 rue Pierre Joigneaux, 21190
Meursault. Tel 03 80 21 23 23;
fax 03 80 21 29 10. ⒻⒻ
This restored 18th-century
mansion, in the centre of
Meursault, is comfortable,
peaceful and well decorated.

Le Montrachet ⒽⓇ
Place des Marronniers, 21190
Puligny-Montrachet. Tel 03 80
21 30 06; fax 03 80 21 39 06.

ⒻⒻ
Reasonable but comfortable
rooms. The restaurant has a very
good wine list and the wine is
served by a talented sommelier.

Le Terroir Ⓡ
Place Jet d'Eau, 21590 Santenay.
Tel 03 80 20 63 47; fax 03 80 20
66 45. Ⓕ
Friendly bistro in the centre of
the village run by a husband and
wife team. Good wine list.

Hostellerie du Vieux Moulin
ⒽⓇ
21420 Bouilland. Tel 03 80 21
51 18; fax 03 80 21 59 90.
ⒻⒻⒻ
Modern rooms in a new annexe
complement imaginative
cooking by Jean-Pierre Silva in
this converted mill in the scenic
Rhoin Valley beyond Savigny.
Leisurely service and a very good
wine list. It's worth going in the
autumn when game is in season.

Wines and Wine Villages

The Côte de Beaune produces two-thirds red wine but is
famous mainly for its white wines, especially those from
the three villages of Meursault, Puligny and Chassagne.

Aloxe-Corton AC   The
village of Aloxe-Corton
(pronounced 'Aloze') nestles
beneath the south-east side of
the Corton hill. It has the largest
amount of Grand Cru land
anywhere in the Côte d'Or.

The Corton and Corton-
Charlemagne Grands Crus,
shared with the communes of
Ladoix and Pernand-Vergelesses,
occupy most of the land on the
steep slope, while the vineyards
further down on the flatter land
qualify for the village AC only.

Corton is the only red Grand
Cru in the Côte de Beaune – the
wine is the firmest of all the
Beaune reds, with an almost
metallic harshness and austerity

when young and should take 10
years to mature. There is very
little white Corton.

Corton-Charlemagne, the
largest white Grand Cru in
Burgundy, lies at the top of the
Corton slope, where the first of
the Côte de Beaune limestone
outcrops becomes apparent. It
can produce firm, full wines, like
Corton, needing at least a decade
to mature. When young, the
wines are austere and steely,
almost with a suggestion of
Chablis, but they develop a
marvellous, creamy richness.

Some of the best Corton and
Corton-Charlemagne producers
live outside Aloxe-Corton and
the best Beaune merchants have

significant holdings on the hill
also. There are 9 Premiers Crus
but relatively little wine is
produced. The village and
Premier Cru vineyards produce
mainly red wine: fullish and
well-coloured but sometimes a
bit solid and earthy.
*Best producers: Maurice Chapuis,
LATOUR, Comte Senard.*

Auxey-Duresses AC   Tucked
away in a little side valley up in
the hills behind Meursault,
Auxey can produce good-value
if never great wines, especially in
a hot vintage. Both red and white
are made. There are 9 Premiers
Crus, the best of which are les
Duresses and Clos du Val.
*Best producers: Alain Craisefond,
Jean-Pierre Diconne, Bernard
Labry, Henri Latour, Michel
Prunier, Philippe Prunier-Damy,
Domaine Roy.*

Beaune AC   As well as being
Burgundy's wine capital, Beaune
is the largest wine commune in
the Côte d'Or and produces a
great deal of reliable, fruity red
wine. This is lighter than
Pommard but not quite so fine
as Volnay. There is a small
amount of white wine.

Much of what would be
perfectly good vineyard land at
the bottom of the slope is now
occupied by the town's suburbs
and the local football pitches.
The 41 Premiers Crus are
divided by the road that leads up

*The Premier Cru of les Duresses is
one of Auxey-Duresses' best
vineyards.*

to Bligny and Bouze-lès-Beaune. Many are in sole ownership of the local merchants, who are the major owners of Beaune's vineyards. The best Premiers Crus are Teurons, Grèves, Cras, Bressandes, Fèves, Vignes-Franches and Clos des Mouches. *Best producers:* BOUCHARD PÈRE ET FILS, *Camille-Giroud, Chanson, Drouhin,* JADOT, LATOUR, *Maison Champy,* MOROT, *Remoissenet.*

Blagny AC This is a little hamlet tucked away quietly in the hills between Meursault and Puligny. As on the Corton hill, Chardonnay is planted on the top of the slope and Pinot Noir lower down. Most of the wine is white and is sold as Puligny-Montrachet or Meursault-Blagny. The Blagny AC covers red wines only. These are not often seen but they are worth searching out as they can be good value. *Best producers:* AMPEAU, LOUIS LATOUR *(Meursault-Blagny), Matrot.*

Chassagne-Montrachet AC Chassagne, like most villages in the Côte d'Or, used to be a red-wine village but now its reputation is for Chardonnay not Pinot Noir. In 1879, at the same time as neighbouring Puligny, it added the name of its most famous vineyard to its own. Its half of the Montrachet and Bâtard-Montrachet Grands Crus, and the tiny Criots-Bâtard-Montrachet (see Puligny-Montrachet p.48 for further description), lie north of the main N6 road but most of Chassagne's other vineyards are to the south, with the majority of the 52 Premiers Crus on the same level as a dominant marble quarry.

South of the village, the higher slopes produce almost entirely white wine – les Caillerets, Grandes-Ruchottes, la Romanée, la Grande-Montagne and les Embrazées are the best. The lower slopes (these can all call themselves Morgeots, and usually do, rather than invoking a more precise but less well-known name) yield both red and

white wine. Above the village, Clos St-Jean is a red wine Premier Cru for the most part, while further north, Chardonnay is planted on the upper slopes – les Chaumées and les Vergers – and Pinot Noir lower down in les Chenevottes and les Macherelles. Adjoining the Grands Crus, the Premiers Crus of En Rémilly, Blanchots-Dessous and Vide-Bourse produce fine, but rarely seen white wines.

The whites are better and more popular than the reds and sell for twice as much. They are firm, full wines, although occasionally a little solid. Red Chassagne can be plump with fruit and good value but, like the white, it is sometimes a little earthy and solid and tends not to mature gracefully.

Orchards share the land with vineyards in the Hautes-Côtes de Beaune, here at Nantoux.

Best producers: Guy Amiot, Blain-Gagnard, Colin-Deléger, Fontaine-Gagnard, JEAN-NOËL GAGNARD, GAGNARD-DELAGRANGE, *Marquis de Laguiche (wines made and bottled by Drouhin in Beaune), Bernard Morey, Michel Niellon, various members of the Pillot family, Ramonet.*

Chorey-lès-Beaune AC Chorey lies on the 'wrong', i.e. east, side of the N74, the main Beaune-Dijon road, as do most of its vineyards, which are chiefly Pinot Noir. There are no Premiers Crus and most of the wine is sold as Côte de Beaune-Villages. The village wine is soft, early-maturing Pinot: a good

introduction to more serious red Burgundy. *Best producers:* CH. DE CHOREY (JACQUES GERMAIN), *Tollot-Beaut.*

Côte de Beaune-Villages AC This is a general AC for red wine from 16 villages up and down the Côte. Nowadays most producers prefer to sell their wine under individual village names.

Grands Crus The Côte de Beaune has fewer Grands Crus than the Côte de Nuits and, apart from Corton, they are all for white wine. But such is the world renown of these white Grands Crus that it is easy to forget that the Côte de Beaune, in fact, makes more red wine than white. The Grands Crus account for about 11 per cent of all wine produced in the Côte de Beaune.

They are listed below by village. For further descriptions, see the individual village entries in this section.
Aloxe-Corton and Ladoix-Serrigny
Corton (105ha)
Aloxe-Corton, Ladoix-Serrigny and Pernand-Vergelesses
Corton-Charlemagne (52ha)
Puligny-Montrachet
Bienvenues-Bâtard-Montrachet (3.7ha), Chevalier-Montrachet (7.4ha)
Puligny-Montrachet and Chassagne-Montrachet
Le Montrachet (8ha), Bâtard-Montrachet (11.9ha).
Chassagne-Montrachet
Criots-Bâtard-Montrachet (1.6ha)

Hautes-Côtes de Beaune AC The Hautes-Côtes de Beaune vineyards are split into two groups: the southern, much larger one is between Nantoux and Marcheseuil near Nolay over the *départementale* border in the Saône-et-Loire. The second is between Echevronne north of Pernand-Vergelesses and the borders of the Hautes-Côtes de Nuits at Magny-lès-Villers. Other wine villages in the Hautes-Côtes de Beaune are Mavilly-Mandelot, Orches, Nolay, Change and Paris l'Hôpital.

The landscape is more undulating with fewer woods and more vineyards than in the

Hautes-Côtes de Nuits. There is also some mixed farming (cows and sheep as well as cereals). Many growers are members of the local co-operative, les Caves des Hautes-Côtes, which has its headquarters outside Beaune. The wines are both red and white and they are significantly better in hot years.
Best producers: *Claude Cornu (Magny-lès-Villers), Lucien Jacob (Echevronne), Jean-Baptiste Joliot (Nantoux), Claude Nouveau (Marcheseuil).*

Ladoix AC Tucked under the eastern side of the Corton hill, the village of Ladoix-Serrigny is the most northerly commune in the Côte de Beaune. As well as a small part of the Corton Grand Cru (see Aloxe-Corton p.46) there are 7 Premiers Crus – 4 join onto Corton and the remainder lie across the D115 on a south-facing slope. Much of the remaining wine from Ladoix goes under the Côte de Beaune-Villages label. Village Ladoix wine is a light-coloured red and is and often a little lean, but the local growers are making progress.
Best producers: *Prince Florent de Mérode.*

Maranges AC This relatively new AC is the most southerly one in the Côte d'Or. It is a continuation of the Santenay AC as the slope bends round, facing south, through the villages of Dezize, Sampigny and Cheilly. There are 6 Premiers Crus, and if the wine does not come from one of these vineyards it may well be sold as Côte de Beaune-Villages. Most of the wines are red, attractive and medium-bodied. There is a little light white.
Best producers: *Bernard Bachelet et Fils, Fernand Chevrot, Contat-Grange, Edmond Monnot.*

Meursault AC Along with Puligny and Chassagne, the large village of Meursault is one of the 'great three' making up the heartland of Chardonnay in the Côte de Beaune. There are no Grands Crus but to compensate,

there is a great cluster of Premiers Crus (14 in all). Continuing northward from Puligny, the line of Premiers Crus comes to an end at Goutte d'Or. Above and beyond lie parcels of vineyard which used to be unofficial Deuxièmes Crus before the days of official classifications. This concept is still valid here, since the wines from these vineyards, for example, Narvaux, Tillets and Tessons, are much better than those from vineyards down on the flatter land below.

Straight white Meursault is a round, ample wine with a nutty, buttery background. There is a little red, produced on the Volnay side, below the vineyard of Santenots (which growers are allowed to sell as Volnay). The red sold as Meursault, from the lower slopes, tends to be a little dense.
Best producers: *Robert Ampeau, Michel Bouzereau, Boyer-Martenot,* COCHE-DURY, *Patrick Javillier,* FRANÇOIS JOBARD, COMTES LAFON, PIERRE MOREY, ROULOT.

The cellars of Domaine Comtes Lafon in Meursault are some of the deepest and coldest in Burgundy.

Monthélie AC This mainly red wine village lies halfway along the Côte de Beaune between Volnay and Auxey-Duresses. Most of its better vineyards lie above the village on the extension of the Volnay slope, facing almost due south. The red wine can be very good value: Volnay-ish at half the

price. The small amount of white produced is clean and fruity, and is also good value. There are 11 Premiers Crus.
Best producers: *Darviot-Perrin, Paul Garaudet, Monthélie-Douhairet.*

Pernand-Vergelesses AC Pernand is an attractive village clutching the side of a hill facing the western side of the Corton hill. Apart from Pernand's share of the Corton-Charlemagne Grand Cru (see Aloxe-Corton p.46), the best vineyards continue round the slopes beneath the Bois Noël toward Santenay. The prized possession is the Île de Vergelesses, a contender for promotion from Premier to Grand Cru. There are 4 other Premiers Crus.

Pernand produces mainly red wines, a little leaner than those of Aloxe-Corton as most of the vineyards face west or even north-west, but they are often more graceful because they have better acidity. Perhaps because of the long-winded village name, they are hard to sell and consequently are good value.
Best producers: *Bonneau du Martray, Dubreuil-Fontaine, Roland Rupet.*

Pommard AC Pommard lies between Beaune and Volnay, and in total contrast to these two ACs, the wines are big and sturdy. There are 24 Premiers Crus, lying either on the gentler-sloping Beaune side, for example les Epenots, or on the steeper, rocky Volnay flank, for example les Rugiens.
Best producers: COMTE ARMAND, *Jean-Marc Boillot, de Courcel, Parent, Rebourgeon-Muré.*

Premiers Crus This category of vineyard is the next one down from Grands Crus and there is a grand total of 339 in the Côte de Beaune. Some of these Premiers Crus are very obscure and have the right to be sold under a better known name. For instance, the name of the Morgeots vineyard in Chassagne can be used by 20 of its immediate neighbours. The

Premier Cru land will normally occupy the middle of the slope, protected from the prevailing wind by the hill behind, exposed to the south-west in order to enjoy maximum sun, and where the drainage is at its best.

The Côte de Beaune has only one red Grand Cru, Corton. The leading red Premiers Crus are the best part of Pommard's Epenots, les Rugiens Bas and the best of the Volnays (Clos des Chênes, Taillepieds, the top part of Caillerets). Of the white Premiers Crus, Meursault's Perrières Dessous is the best. Before the *appellation contrôlée* system was introduced in 1936, the concept of Deuxième Cru was widespread. It is still valid in Meursault.

Puligny-Montrachet AC
This village is the greatest Chardonnay commune in the world. Two of the 5 local Grands Crus lie entirely within its boundaries: Chevalier-Montrachet and Bienvenues-Bâtard-Montrachet. Montrachet and Bâtard-Montrachet are divided between Puligny and Chassagne. Only the diminutive Criots-Bâtard-Montrachet lies entirely within Chassagne.

Of these Grands Crus Montrachet is clearly head and shoulders above the others, by virtue of the wine's sheer concentration, breeding and ability to age. Further up the slope, Chevalier's higher elevation and stonier soil produce powerful, minerally wine almost as concentrated, with splendid fruit and balance. Bâtard, on heavier soil, can be a little solid, while Bienvenues and Criots (in Chassagne) are lighter and more flowery. All can age for at least 10 years.

There are 24 Premiers Crus, of which the best – Pucelles, Combattes, Caillerets – are on the same line as the Grands Crus. The village produces almost entirely white wine: crisper, more peachy than that of Meursault, better-balanced and more complete than that of Chassagne. Sometimes these can be delicious when they are

young, but in good vintages they can age better than any other Chardonnays. The Grands Crus, particularly, need at least 5 years in bottle, preferably 10.
Best producers: CARILLON, *Clerc, Ch. de Puligny-Montrachet,* DOMAINE LEFLAIVE, *Olivier Leflaive Frères, Paul Pernot,* SAUZET.

Tucked into the slope above its vineyards the small village of Volnay is famous for its perfumed red wines.

St-Aubin AC The St-Aubin vineyards overlook the main N6 road as it snakes its way up into the Hautes-Côtes. A high proportion of the land is classified as Premier Cru (there are 29) but, while producing an agreeable lesser-Puligny style of white wine, especially in hot years, these are not in the same league as Puligny's own Premiers Crus. But then they are less expensive and mature earlier.

Two-thirds of the wine is red and good-value if somewhat light in style. The hamlet of Gamay is included in the AC.
Best producers: Gilles Bouton, Marc Colin, Hubert Lamy, Larue, Henri Prudhon et Fils, Gérard Thomas.

St-Romain AC Perched up in the hills behind Auxey-Duresses, St-Romain's vineyards lie spread out on the slopes below the village. There are no Premiers Crus and the wine is a sort of halfway house between those of the Hautes-Côtes and the main villages of the Côte de Beaune. The whites, crisp, clean, fruity and for reasonably early drinking, are more interesting

than the reds. The region's main cooper, or *tonnelier*, François Frères is based here. The use of new oak is increasingly fashionable, and the best wood is air-dried for 3 years. You will see great piles of it outside the François premises.
Best producers: d'Auvernay, Alain Gras, Thierry Guyot.

Santenay AC Santenay is a large, mainly red-wine village at the southern end of the Côte. There are 13 Premiers Crus, of which the best lie to the north near the boundary with Chassagne-Montrachet. Most of the wines are medium-bodied reds, with an underlying firmness and good meaty fruit; they can be good value.
Best producers: Joseph Belland, Philippe Brenot, VINCENT GIRARDIN, *Louis Lequin, René Lequin-Colin, Lucien Muzard.*

Savigny-lès-Beaune AC
This large village is split in two by the Rhoin river which flows east out of the Hautes-Côtes, so some of the vineyards face as much north as east. The most elegant wines come from the other side of the valley where the vineyards face south. There are 22 Premiers Crus. The wines are mainly red: medium- to medium-full bodied, with good fruit and staying power. They are good value.
Best producers: SIMON BIZE, *Lucien Camus-Brochon,* CHANDON DE BRIAILLES, *Maurice Ecard, Jean-Marc Pavelot.*

Volnay AC Volnay is the best-known red-wine village of the Côte de Beaune, producing wines that may only be medium-bodied but which have few rivals in the complexity of their perfume and elegance. More than half the vineyards are Premiers Crus (there are 33), including Santenots, whose wines are labelled as Volnay, although the vineyard itself lies across the boundary in Meursault.
Best producers: MARQUIS D'ANGERVILLE, *Yvon Clerget,* MICHEL LAFARGE, HUBERT DE MONTILLE, *Pousse d'Or.*

At Montagny-lès-Buxy in the far south of the Côte Chalonnaise, only the well-drained, better-exposed slopes are planted with vines. In the Montagny appellation some 53 vineyards have been designated Premier Cru. As in the Côte d'Or, these better Premier Cru vineyards are found in mid-slope where they have adequate protection from the prevailing westerly winds but still benefit from superior drainage and are better angled to the sun than those vineyards down at the foot of the slope. The appellation covers white wines only, from Chardonnay. Notice in the middle distance to the left, a vineyard which is being allowed to lie fallow for a couple of years before being replanted. Below it, the white pickets and absence of dense growth indicate a newly planted vineyard.

Warm, sunny weather in September can make all the difference to the quality of the grape harvest, here at Montagny-lès-Buxy in the southern Côte Chalonnaise.

Map illustrations: (above) baskets of Chardonnay grapes; (centre) Ch. de Rully; (below) vineyards in the Mercurey appellation.

TOUR SUMMARY

Starting in the north at Chagny, the tour covers the wine villages of the Côte Chalonnaise, which roughly follow the line of the D981 road south to Cluny.

Distance covered 25km (15 miles).

Time needed 2 hours.

Terrain The tour uses main and *départementale* roads that are easy to drive.

Hotels Chalon-sur-Saône is the largest city in Burgundy after Dijon and offers a comprehensive range of hotels. But wine lovers are better off staying in Chagny or in the wine villages.

Restaurants One of France's top restaurants, Lameloise, is in Chagny. Otherwise there are plenty of simple bistros in the wine villages.

Côte Chalonnaise

In many ways the Côte Chalonnaise is the younger sister of the Côte d'Or: the wines, both red and white, are made from mainly Pinot Noir and Chardonnay, but they are lighter with less body and are ready for drinking earlier. Until recently much of the crop was sold simply as Burgundy, without any more specific appellation. Near Santenay, just west of Chagny, the relatively unbroken slope of the Côte d'Or peters out; heading south toward Cluny the Côte Chalonnaise is made up of intermittent hills, offering only occasional shelter from the westerly winds, and occasional sloping land angled toward the sun. In the main, the scattered vineyards slope down toward the D981, the road that connects Chagny with Cluny in the Mâconnais.

The countryside is less uniform than further north – woodland and pasture on the more exposed land alternate with outcrops of vineyards, which are located on any suitable south- and south-east-facing slopes. There are some charming villages and plenty of rural *auberges* and bistros. The local growers, because they have to try a bit harder to sell their wine, are more welcoming to passing visitors and the wines can be good value.

As well as the relatively recent regional appellation, Bourgogne-Côte Chalonnaise, there are four village appellations: Rully, Mercurey and Givry for both red and white wines and Montagny for whites only. Rully is also a centre for sparkling wine, and the best Aligoté wine in Burgundy traditionally comes from the village of Bouzeron which has its own appellation, Bourgogne Aligoté de Bouzeron.

Although the Chalonnaise is further south than the Côte d'Or, and the vineyards lie at approximately the same altitude, it is cooler, and getting enough sun to ripen the grapes can be a problem. The soil, though similarly based on limestone, is less exposed and rocky and it takes longer to warm up during the day. The harvest takes place a week or so later and as a consequence the wines are never as richly concentrated or as full bodied as they are further north. Much of the lesser wine is used for Crémant de Bourgogne.

The Tour

Set out from Chagny on the D974 in the direction of le Creusot, Remigny and Santenay. Then take the narrow D219 under the railway bridge toward the sleepy hamlet of Bouzeron, crossing the Canal du Centre, which connects the Loire with the Saône rivers.

The northernmost wine village in the Côte Chalonnaise, Bouzeron has traditionally been a centre for Aligoté, but here, and throughout the region, the vine is under fierce

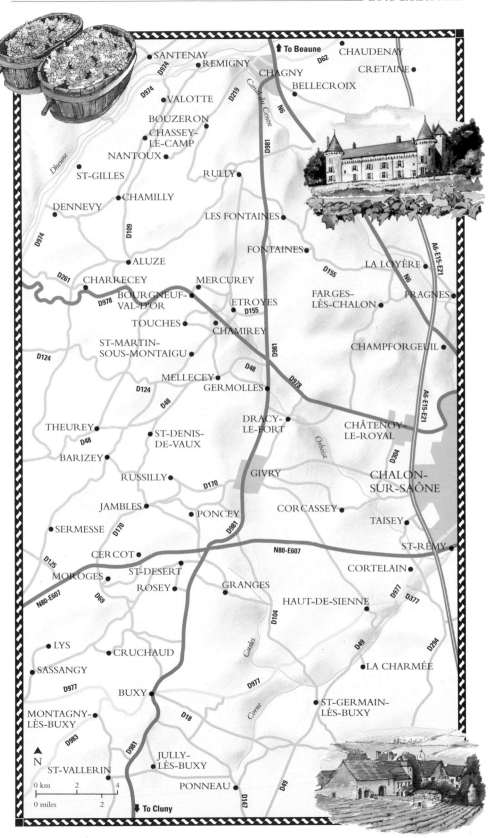

SANTENAY
REMIGNY
To Beaune
CHAUDENAY
CHAGNY
CRETAINE
BELLECROIX
D62
D974
D974
VALOTTE
D219
N6
D981
BOUZERON
CHASSEY-
LE-CAMP
NANTOUX
RULLY
Dheune
ST-GILLES
CHAMILLY
DENNEVY
LES FONTAINES
D109
D974
FONTAINES
ALUZE
LA LOYÈRE
A6-E15-E21
D261
CHARRECEY
MERCUREY
D155
N6
BOURGNEUF-
VAL-D'OR
ETROYES
D155
FARGES-
LÈS-CHALON
FRAGNES
D978
TOUCHES
CHAMIREY
ST-MARTIN-
SOUS-MONTAIGU
D124
CHAMPFORGEUIL
D981
MELLECEY
D48
GERMOLLES
D978
A6-E15-E21
D124
D48
THEUREY
ST-DENIS-
DE-VAUX
DRACY-
LE-FORT
CHÂTENOY-
LE-ROYAL
D48
Orbise
BARIZEY
D304
RUSSILLY
GIVRY
CHALON-
SUR-SAÔNE
D170
JAMBLES
PONCEY
CORCASSEY
TAISEY
SERMESSE
D170
D981
CERCOT
N80-E607
ST-RÉMY
D125
ST-DESERT
CORTELAIN
MOROGES
ROSEY
GRANGES
D977
D377
N80-E607
D69
HAUT-DE-SIENNE
D104
D49
D294
LYS
CRUCHAUD
Guiles
SASSANGY
LA CHARMÉE
D977
D977
BUXY
ST-GERMAIN-
LÈS-BUXY
MONTAGNY-
LÈS-BUXY
D18
Corne
D983
D981
N
ST-VALLERIN
JULLY-
LÈS-BUXY
0 km   2   4
PONNEAU
D49
0 miles   2
To Cluny
D147

competition from other crops. Fields full of the local, dun-coloured Charollais beef cattle are interspersed with ones of maize, and vines are planted wherever the slopes face south-east and are protected from the prevailing westerly winds. The best grower in Bouzeron, which has long been known for its Aligoté wine, is Aubert de Villaine who is also a director of the world-famous Domaine de la Romanée-Conti in Vosne-Romanée.

From Bouzeron take another minor road over the hills south to Rully, past the Montagne de la Folie which divides the two villages. At the top there is a wonderful view of Rully and its vineyards below, and the distinctive slate turrets of the medieval Ch. de Rully can also be seen. This would be a good place for a picnic. The castle belongs to Antonin Rodet, the most important local wine merchant, who is based in Mercurey. To the left, at the northern end of the ridge, is a water tower which dominates the land-scape. It lies in the middle of one of Rully's best estates, Domaine de la Folie owned by Xavier Noël-Bouton. To the right, the Rully vineyards merge into those of Mercurey.

Rully is an attractive small village which was originally famous for its Crémant de Bourgogne but now concentrates more on still white wines – a foil to the reds of neighbour-ing Mercurey and Givry. The still whites, increasingly aged in oak, are crisp, fresh and aromatic, with a Victoria plum flavour, while the reds are light with an attractive cherry and strawberry fruit.

Turn south at the church in Rully and take the sign-posted road through the vineyards over the hill toward Mercurey. Straddling the D978, the main road from Chalon to Autun, Mercurey is the largest wine village in the Côte Chalonnaise and nearly all its wine is red; it is the sturdiest and longest-lasting of all Chalonnais wines. The vineyards lie on a south-facing slope, which extends east and west for several kilometres, as well as south toward St-Martin-sous-Montaigu. Mercurey's best-known Premier Cru, Voyens, lies above the village on the south-facing slopes of a hill where there was once a Gallo-Roman temple dedicated to the god Mercury, from which the village gets its name. There is now a windmill on the site.

Mercurey has some substantial houses, a good hotel/restaurant, the Val d'Or and a Maison du Vin located in the Ch. de Garnerot on a hill overlooking the vineyards. There are a number of important local wine estates. The excellent Nuits-St-Georges merchant Joseph Faiveley owns a 40ha estate here. Antonin Rodet, another very good merchant, is based in Mercurey and looks after the neighbouring Ch. de Chamirey estate as well as that of Ch. de Rully; Michel Juillot and his cousin Émile are two more good producers to look out for in Mercurey.

The village of Rully made its reputation with sparkling wine but is now as well known for its good-value red and white wines.

From Mercurey take the D978 toward Châlon, turn right to Chamirey and its château and then on to St-Martin-sous-Montaigu. Turn left toward Mellecey and join the D981 at Germolles, where the 12th-century château can be visited. Continue south through woodland and fields of Charollais cattle to the little town of Givry. This used to be the wine centre for the whole area but today it has become a prosperous commuter feeder town for the nearby industrial city of Châlon.

Givry, as all the local wines proudly declare, was the preferred wine of King Henri IV. The soil here just begins to change from the marl and chalky limestone of the northern part of Burgundy to the richer, more sandy limestone of the Mâconnais. As in Mercurey, there is a little clay and the wines are predominantly red with an intensity of fruit and ability to age that is unusual for the Côte Chalonnaise. The small amount of white has improved considerably in recent years and, from a reliable producer, can be good value. Givry's vineyards follow the arc of the hills as they curve around from above the town down toward Jambles, a distance of about 5km (3 miles). There are 20 Premiers Crus. Some of the best-known estates include Clos Salomon, whose records date back to the 14th century, and the estates of Joblot, the brothers Lumpp and Baron Thénard, owner of important parcels in Montrachet and other Côte d'Or vineyards, as well as a substantial vineyard here.

Leave Givry on the D170 and head south-west toward Russilly and Jambles. Both of these pretty, sleepy villages are home to good local growers such as Vincent Lumpp and René Bourgeon in Jambles. Return to the D981 through Poncey.

Based in Mercurey, Antonin Rodet is a large merchant owning or controlling some fine estates in the Côte d'Or as well as the Côte Chalonnaise.

As you cross the N80, the main Châlon to le Creusot road, the Givry vineyards come to an end, and there is a short gap before reaching the white-wine appellation of Montagny, whose vineyards are in Buxy and neighbouring Montagny-lès-Buxy, Jully-lès-Buxy and St Vallerin. As the name suggests, the village of Montagny lies on a little hill above its vineyards, as does Jully. There is an important co-operative at Buxy, which makes much of the local wine – and to a very high standard. Montagny wines used to be bone-dry and rather lean but, with better wine-making and the judicious use of new oak, they are now rather more softly toasty Chardonnays, with a little more body and acidity than other Côte Chalonnaise whites, and good value.

Carry on to Montagny, Jully and St-Vallerin, then back to Buxy. Montagny and Jully are pretty villages with vineyards running down the slopes below them, and picturesque views from the top. St Vallerin, like so many in the area, has an attractive Romanesque church. Return direct to Chagny by the D981, or make a detour to visit Châlon.

Côte Chalonnaise Fact File

The main tourist centres are Chagny and Châlon-sur-Saône, a large industrial town and inland port, but neither is a true wine town like Beaune or Nuits-St-Georges.

Information
Office du Tourisme
Boulevard de la République, 71000 Châlon-sur-Saône. Tel 03 85 48 37 97; fax 03 85 48 63 55.

Office du Tourisme
2 rue des Halles, 71150 Chagny. Tel 03 85 87 25 95; fax 03 85 87 14 44.

BIVB
12 boulevard Bretonnière, 21204 Beaune. Tel 03 80 25 04 80; fax 03 80 25 04 81.
Wine information, maps and lists of growers to visit in the Côte Chalonnaise as well as elsewhere in Burgundy.

Markets
Chagny – Sunday morning
Châlon-sur-Saône – Friday
    morning

Where to Buy Wine
As elsewhere in Burgundy, most growers offer opportunities to taste and buy their wines, but choose carefully.
Cave des Vignerons de Buxy
Les Vignes de la Croix, 71390 Buxy. Tel 03 85 92 03 03; fax 03 85 92 08 06.
The standard of wines at this large, modern co-operative is high. The specialities are the Montagny and Côte Chalonnaise wines.

Maison du Vin
Picard Bourgognes, route de St-Loup de la Salle, 71150 Chagny. Tel 03 65 87 51 00; fax 03 85 87 51 11.
Wine information bureau-cum-shop-cum-mini museum owned by one of the region's local merchants.

Maison des Vins de la Côte Chalonnaise
Promenade Ste-Marc, 71100 Châlon-sur-Saône. Tel 03 85 41 64 00; restaurant 85 41 66 66; fax 03 85 41 99 83.

Wine information, maps and lists of cellars to visit in the Côte Chalonnaise. Local wines are on sale and there is a restaurant.

Maison du Vin de Mercurey
Ch. de Garnerot, 71640 Mercurey. Tel 03 85 45 22 99; fax 03 85 45 24 88.
Information on the wines of Mercurey, plus local wines on sale.

Festivals and Events
The Châlon Wine Carnival takes place for a week at the end of February.

Where to Stay and Eat
Auberge des Alouettes ®
1 route de Givry, 71880 Châtenoy-le-Royal. Tel 03 85 48 32 15; fax 03 85 93 12 96. Ⓕ
On the D69 on the outskirts of Châlon, this *auberge* has a number of menus at various prices. Reasonable wine list.

Auberge du Camp Romain Ⓗ Ⓡ
71150 Chassey-le-Camp. Tel 03 85 87 09 91; fax 03 85 87 11 51. Ⓕ Ⓕ
Quiet, elegant hotel west of Chagny with a reasonable restaurant. Swimming pool.

Hostellerie Château de Bellecroix Ⓗ Ⓡ
Route de Châlon, 71150 Chagny. Tel 03 85 87 13 86; fax 03 85 91 28 62. Ⓕ Ⓕ
A quiet, luxurious hotel created out of a Victorian folly. Good restaurant and wine list. Swimming-pool.

Le Dracy Ⓗ Ⓡ
71640 Dracy-le-Fort. Tel 03 85 87 81 81; fax 03 85 87 77 49. Ⓕ Ⓕ
Comfortable hotel among vineyards near Givry with park, tennis court, terrace and swimming pool. Unambitious restaurant.

Girardot ®
71390 Buxy. Tel 03 85 92 04 04. Ⓕ
Simple local restaurant near the co-operative. You can eàt outside in fine weather.

Halle Ⓗ Ⓡ
Place Halle, 71640 Givry. Tel 03 85 44 32 45; fax 03 85 44 49 45. Ⓕ Ⓕ
Simple and unpretentious bistro. There are 7 bedrooms.

Lameloise Ⓗ Ⓡ
36 place d Armes, 71150 Chagny. Tel 03 85 87 08 85; fax 03 85 87 03 87. Ⓕ Ⓕ Ⓕ
The best place to eat, by far, within striking distance of Beaune and, indeed, rated one of the best restaurants in France. Excellent food and masterful wine list. Comfortable rooms.

Moulin de Martorey Ⓗ Ⓡ
71100 St-Rémy. Tel 03 85 48 12 98; fax 03 85 48 73 67. Ⓕ Ⓕ
This converted mill with a fine garden is near the Châlon Sud *autoroute* exit, yet is peaceful enough. It offers the best food in the neighbourhood and the cheapest menu is excellent value. There is a splendid wine list.

Relais de Montagny Ⓗ
71390 Buxy. Tel 03 85 92 19 90; fax 03 85 92 07 19. Ⓕ Ⓕ
Comfortable, modern hotel with swimming-pool. The Girardot is under the same management.

Hôtellerie du Val d'Or Ⓗ Ⓡ
Grande-Rue, 71640 Mercurey. Tel 03 85 45 13 70; fax 03 85 45 18 45. Ⓕ Ⓕ
Long-established, comfortable, good-value hotel in the centre. The restaurant is very good and the wine list includes plenty of good local growers.

Le Vendangerot Ⓗ Ⓡ
71150 Rully. Tel 03 85 87 20 09; fax 03 85 91 27 18. Ⓕ
In Rully's main square, this simple but welcoming restaurant concentrates on local regional food. The wine list is reasonable. There are 12 bedrooms.

Wines and Wine Villages

The five village ACs run conveniently south from Chagny in rolling countryside west of the Saône river. The village of Bouzeron specializes in Aligoté wine.

Bourgogne-Côte Chalonnaise AC Spiralling wine prices in the Côte d'Or just to the north and improving quality in the Côte Chalonnaise led to the creation of this new regional AC in 1990. Before then the wines were labelled simply Bourgogne. The AC covers red wines from Pinot Noir and whites from Chardonnay and Aligoté and is rapidly gaining a good reputation.

Being the coolest part of Burgundy, the wines are lighter and more forward than those of the Côte d'Or, as well as less rich and sturdy than those of the Mâconnais. They are proportionately better, therefore, in the better vineyards.
Best producers: Cave des Vignerons de Buxy (Buxy), DE VILLAINE *(Bouzeron).*

Bouzeron This is the only village in Burgundy to have an AC for its Aligoté, the main reason being that the variety has all but disappeared – or has been relegated to less good vineyards – elsewhere in Burgundy. Pinot Noir and Chardonnay grown here qualify for the regional Bourgogne-Côte Châlonnaise AC. This is a new vineyard area and in good hands the wines are delicious and inexpensive.
Best producers: BOUCHARD PÈRE ET FILS, *Chanzy Frères, de Villaine.*

Buxy The village of Buxy within the Montagny appellation is well known for its large co-operative which is one of the best in the whole of Burgundy (see p.56).

Givry AC Like the village of Mercurey, Givry produces mainly red wines, but only about a third as much. As in Rully, the main expanse of Givry's vineyards faces south-east toward the D981. Many of the 20 Premiers Crus are in sole

ownership. The red wines are a little lighter than those of Mercurey, but can be very elegant and fragrant.
Best producers: René Bourgeon, du Gardin, JEAN-MARC JOBLOT, *Laborde-Juillot, François Lumpp, Vincent Lumpp, Ragot, Thénard.*

Mercurey AC Mercurey is the most important wine village in the Côte Chalonnaise, and the whole area was historically known as the Région de Mercurey. The AC produces almost entirely red wine. It is the fullest of the Chalonnaise reds, well-coloured, rich, meaty and plummy, and can age well in bottle. There are 27 Premiers Crus, many of which are in sole ownership.
Best producers: FAIVELEY *(Domaine la Croix Jacquelet), Émile Juillot,* MICHEL JUILLOT, *Guy Narjoux,* ANTONIN RODET, *Saier.*

ownership. The red wines are a anomaly has now been amended and the best vineyard sites have been formally classified as Premiers Crus. There are now no fewer than 53 Premiers Crus. Most of the wine is made by the excellent co-operative at Buxy. Montagny is a solid sort of white wine, usually full and ripe but lacking a little raciness. The recent wider use of new oak has given the wine more personality and it is certainly more dependable than white Rully.
Best producers: Cave des Vignerons de Buxy, Alain Roy-Thévenin (Ch. de la Saule), Steinmaier.

Rully AC Rully makes about two-thirds white wine, much of the least good stuff being used for the local Crémant de Bourgogne. The base wine for Crémant needs to be acidic – rather more so than would be palatable in a still wine. The 23 Premiers Crus lie on the south-east-facing slopes above the village and they produce the most distinctive and elegant Côte Chalonnaise whites,

The village of Bouzeron near Chagny is best known for its Aligoté wine.

Montagny AC This AC extends over 4 villages: Buxy, Montagny, Jully and St-Vallerin, and covers only white wine. Reds made here are sold as Bourgogne-Côte Chalonnaise. Traditionally, all the wines could be called Premier Cru if the grapes had enough sugar in them to yield 11.5° of alcohol. But this

aromatically fruity, with good acidity, for medium-term aging. The reds have tended to be somewhat rustic but are now lighter and fruitier.
Best producers: Raymond Bêtes, Jean-Claude Brelières, la Renarde (Delorme), Raymond Dureuil/ Dureuil-Janthial, la Folie, Henri et Paul Jacqueson.

In the southern Mâconnais the rock of Solutré, an immense limestone cliff, dominates the Pouilly-Fuissé vineyards. The climb up from the village below is arduous but the view from the top is spectacular. In prehistoric times ancient man used to channel herds of local beasts up the hill and over the cliff at the top. A deep ossuary a short distance away above the village testifies to the abundance of life in the locality before the Chardonnay grape took over. The broad swathe of south-facing vineyards catches every last drop of sunshine but the vineyards here also swing around to the north and these ones receive less sun. And so, as elsewhere in Burgundy, the precise location of the vines can be critical to the quality of the final wine.

Gamay grapes are the only ones allowed for red Beaujolais, which can range from a juicy, simple, abundantly fruity wine to something more serious that will age for a few years in bottle.

Map illustrations: (above left) the church at Fuissé; (above right) the Roman martyr, St Amour; (below left) Gamay vines; (below right) the Moulin-à-Vent windmill.

TOUR SUMMARY

Starting at Mâcon, this tour covers the southern Mâconnais region around Pouilly-Fuissé AC, and then moves south into northern Beaujolais, home of the Beaujolais Cru villages.

Distance covered 110km (70 miles).

Time needed 4 hours, excluding detours.

Terrain The tour uses main and *départementale* roads, which can be busy but are otherwise easy to drive.

Hotels Many of the hotels in the region are modest establishments and offer very good value.

Restaurants Most of the restaurants concentrate on local dishes and are very reasonably priced.

Heart of Mâconnais and Beaujolais

West of Mâcon the attractive landscape of lush, rolling hills, vineyards, orchards and red Provençal-tiled farmhouses is more reminiscent of Mediterranean France than of the heart of Burgundy further north. With higher temperatures and occasional storms, the southern Mâconnais climate also marks a transition point between northern and southern France. The vineyards here are almost entirely Chardonnay and the few red wines, sold as Mâcon Rouge, come from Beaujolais' Gamay grape rather than Pinot Noir, the classic red grape of the rest of Burgundy.

The Mâconnais area actually begins much further north at Sennecy-le-Grand, on the Saône river north of Tournus, and runs south, expanding to perhaps 15km (9 miles) in width, confined by the river to the east and a range of hills which run from Sennecy to Cluny and beyond to the west. The best vineyards in this northern part are designated Mâcon-Villages rather than straight Mâcon and much of the wine is made by the local co-operatives – the ones at Lugny, Viré, Clessé and Chardonnay have particularly high reputations. But the best Mâconnais vineyards lie south of the N79, the main road between Mâcon and Cluny: here are the appellations of Pouilly-Fuissé and its satellites: Pouilly-Vinzelles, Pouilly-Loché and St-Véran.

South of St-Véran the Mâconnais vineyards blend almost imperceptibly into those of Beaujolais. Beaujolais is a completely different story again – the hills are of granite rather than of limestone as in the Mâconnais and the wine is almost entirely red, from Gamay. North-west of Belleville the slopes qualify for the Beaujolais-Villages appellation and the top ten wine villages here are called the Beaujolais Crus.

The Tour

Capital of the Saône-et-Loire department, Mâcon is an important wine centre in its own right and a useful base for visiting the region. From the centre, take the N79 west in the direction of Cluny as far as la Croix-Blanche, making sure that at la Roche-Vineuse, after about 9km (5½ miles), you keep to the old road and not the new dual carriageway. This is where you catch your first sight of vineyards and where the wines of Olivier Merlin at the Domaine du Vieux St-Sartin are recommended. The Relais du Mâconnais at la Croix-Blanche is a good place to stop for lunch. From here it is well worth making a short detour to Berzé-la-Ville, where the Romanesque Chapelle aux Moines has spectacular Byzantine wall paintings; or, if time allows, visiting

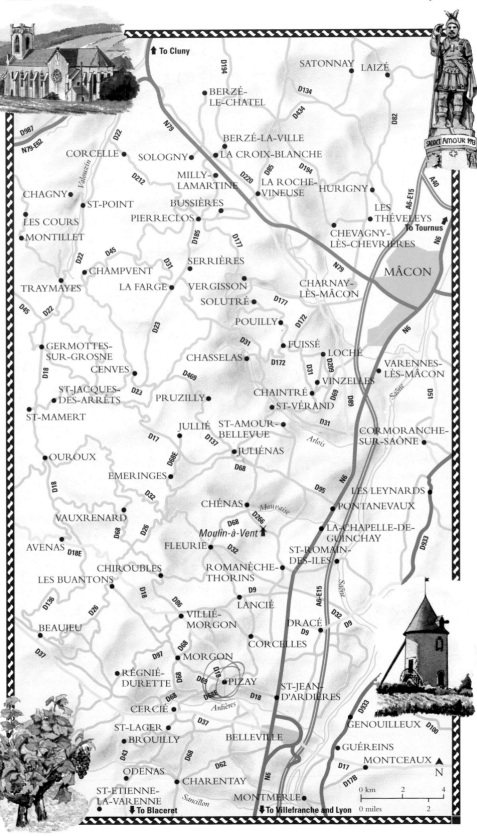

↑ To Cluny

D194

SATONNAY   LAIZÉ

BERZÉ-
LE-CHATEL

D134

D434

D82

D987

D22

N79

BERZÉ-LA-VILLE

CORCELLE   SOLOGNY   LA CROIX-BLANCHE

N79-E52

Valouzin

D212

MILLY-
LAMARTINE

D220

D85

D194

LA ROCHE-
VINEUSE

HURIGNY

A40

A6-E15

CHAGNY   ST-POINT   BUSSIÈRES

LES
THÉVELEYS

LES COURS   PIERRECLOS

To Tournus

MONTILLET

D185

D177

CHEVAGNY-
LÈS-CHEVRIÈRES

N6

D22   D45

CHAMPVENT   SERRIÈRES

D31

N79

MÂCON

TRAYMAYES   LA FARGE   VERGISSON

CHARNAY-
LÈS-MÂCON

D45   D22

SOLUTRÉ   D177

D23

POUILLY   D172

N6

D31

FUISSÉ

GERMOTTES-
SUR-GROSNE

CHASSELAS   D172

LOCHÉ

VARENNES-
LÈS-MÂCON

CENVES

D469

D31

D209

VINZELLES

D18

ST-JACQUES-
DES-ARRÊTS

D23   PRUZILLY

CHAINTRÉ

D69

D89

D51

ST-MAMERT

ST-VÉRAND

D31

CORMORANCHE-
SUR-SAÔNE

OUROUX

JULLIÉ   ST-AMOUR-
BELLEVUE

D17

D137

Arlois

JULIÉNAS

D68E

D68

EMERINGES

D32

N6

D95

LES LEYNARDS

D18

CHÉNAS   Mauvaise   PONTANEVAUX

VAUXRENARD

D68   D266

D68   D26

Moulin-à-Vent ↑

LA-CHAPELLE-DE-
GUINCHAY

AVENAS   D18E

FLEURIE   D32

ST-ROMAIN-
DES-ILES

D933

CHIROUBLES

ROMANÈCHE-
THORINS

LES BUANTONS

D18   D96

D9

A6-E15

Saône

D136   D26

LANCIÉ

VILLIÉ-
MORGON

DRACÉ   D32   D9

BEAUJEU

D68

CORCELLES   D9

D37   D97   MORGON

RÉGNIÉ-
DURETTE

D68   D69   PIZAY

D18

ST-JEAN-
D'ARDIÈRES

D68E

D18

CERCIÉ   Ardières

D933

ST-LAGER   D37

GENOUILLEUX

D100

BROUILLY   BELLEVILLE

D43   D68

GUÉREINS

MONTCEAUX   ▲
N

ODENAS   D62

D17

D17B

ST-ETIENNE-
LA-VARENNE

CHARENTAY

Sancillon   MONTMERLE

N6

0 km   2   4

↓ To Blaceret   ↓ To Villefranche and Lyon   0 miles   2

Cluny a further 10km (6 miles) away. Allow two hours for the total detour. Otherwise, turn left under the dual carriageway and TGV railway line to Milly-Lamartine where Lamartine, the great French author and politician, was born and spent much of his life. Drive on toward Pierreclos where Michel Forest makes good new-woody Pouilly-Fuissé. Beyond the village, the great Vergisson rock looms up ahead with the even more impressive Solutré rock behind it. From Pierreclos take the D177 to Vergisson. Along this road you enter Pouilly-Fuissé, Mâconnais' best-known appellation, which can come from five villages: Vergisson, Solutré, Pouilly, Fuissé and Chaintré (the least good). In Vergisson Guffens-Heynen, Roger Lassarat, Jacques and Nathalie Saumaize and Daniel Barraud are recommended producers.

In the southern Mâconnais the weather is noticeably warmer than in the Côte d'Or, and in the vineyards, basking on the exposed flanks of these well-drained limestone rocks, the grapes have no difficulty in ripening to a high percentage of 13.5 or more. Pouilly-Fuissé is a buttery, creamy wine and the challenge for the winemaker, especially in hot summers, is to keep the wine in balance, preventing it from becoming too heavy.

Vineyards nestle below the dramatic limestone rock of Vergisson and catch every available ray of sunshine.

From Vergisson continue through Solutré (Léger-Plumet is one of the best producers in the village) toward first Pouilly and then Fuissé, passing a neat patchwork of gently sloping vineyards. The views here are particularly good. The Solutré rock is an important archaeological site. Below it remains of prehistoric man and a vast ossuary of the beasts driven over the cliffs were discovered in 1866 and a local museum supplements the main one in Mâcon. Solutré is also a charming village with a local tasting centre, the Caveau de Pouilly-Fuissé and another fine Romanesque church (the whole of southern Mâconnais, the Beaujolais and the Brionnais to the west are immensely rich in the architecture of this period).·

Pouilly is hardly more than a hamlet. Fuissé has a good restaurant, the Au Pouilly-Fuissé, as well as a large number of local growers. The best in this part of the appellation include Ch. Fuissé, Roger Luquet, Ch. de Beauregard, Ferret and Corsin in Fuissé, and Roger Duboeuf in Chaintré.

From Fuissé continue through Loché to Vinzelles. These villages have attached their names to Pouilly to share a bit of the glory – the wine is similar in style to Pouilly-Fuissé but not a patch on its quality. At Vinzelles turn right through Chaintré to St-Vérand. St-Véran – the wine name has no final 'd' – is a relatively new appellation, dating from 1971, and is a useful halfway house between Mâcon Blanc-Villages and Pouilly-Fuissé. Many Pouilly-Fuissé growers also produce St-Veran. St-Vérand is a one-horse place, close your eyes for 10 seconds and you've missed it. There are no growers of note in the village.

At St-Vérand, the southern end of the Mâconnais, the terrain begins to change. The beige crumbly rock of the Mâconnais limestone becomes the greyer grit, sometimes tinged with pink or purple, of Beaujolais granite.

Beaujolais is by far the most prolific of the five Burgundy wine regions. It is some 50km (30 miles) between St-Amour in the north and l'Arbresle on the N7 near Lyon and between the watermeadows of the Saône in the east and the Beaujolais hills in the west it can be as much as 15km (9 miles). In between these four points, on every suitable piece of land, are vines, 99 per cent of them Gamay.

There are three areas within Beaujolais: Beaujolais, Beaujolais-Villages and the Crus. Most of the vineyards for straight Beaujolais, the light, everyday red, are in the south of the region between Villefranche and Lyon in gentle, rolling hills of clay and limestone soil. Much of this wine is also turned into Beaujolais Nouveau to be drunk by Christmas, following the harvest. North of Villefranche the soil is less rich and becomes purer granite, on which Gamay thrives – many of these vineyards are used for the Beaujolais-Villages appellation. Only a little more expensive than basic Beaujolais, Beaujolais-Villages wine is fuller and deeper and much better value for money. Within the Villages area lie the ten Crus. From north to south they are: St-Amour, Juliénas, Chénas, Moulin-à-Vent, Fleurie, Chiroubles, Morgon, Régnié, Brouilly and Côte de Brouilly. The tour passes through all of them.

Vineyards are tightly packed across the hills of northern Beaujolais, where the grapes are now mostly picked by machine rather than by hand.

Leaving St-Vérand and the Mâconnais behind, take the road to St-Amour-Bellevue, named after a Roman soldier martyred here in the fourth century for his Christian beliefs. There is a fine statue of St Amour in the village. The local tasting centre, the Caveau du Cru St-Amour, is in the nearby hamlet of Plâtre-Durand. Local producers to look for include Cave Lamartine and André Poitevin.

Juliénas is the next Cru on the route. Park in the Place du Marché and visit the older of the two churches, which is now the local wine-tasting centre. Pierre Perrachon sells his own wines and various wine items and you can lunch at the Coq au Vin restaurant. Ch. de Juliénas' wine is sold by Georges Duboeuf, whose large firm controls about 10 per cent of the Beaujolais market. Sadly, the château, dating from 1745, is not open to the public, but you can buy the wine at the entrance gateway. The local Cave des Producteurs de Juliénas has a high reputation, as does the Clos de Fief.

Travelling south, Chénas is the next Cru. Daniel Robin's restaurant and the wines of Fernand Charvet at the Domaine des Vieilles Caves and of Hubert Lapierre are recommended. Beyond Chénas on the road to Romanèche-Thorins is the mill of Moulin-à-Vent (there is no village as such). Now closed and shuttered, the old mill stands just off the road and from it there is a good view eastward over the plain of the Saône. The land here seems particularly barren; the grit a touch rosy in colour owing to the presence of manganese. Good local producers include Hubert Lapierre again (many produce both Chénas and Moulin-à-Vent, but prefer to sell the latter, since it usually fetches 25 per cent more) and the Bloud family at the Ch. du Moulin-à-Vent.

Juliénas is a bustling wine village with a tasting centre and many growers selling directly to the public.

Romanèche-Thorins is home to les Maritonnes, a traditional, top-quality hotel and restaurant, and it is also the headquarters of Georges Duboeuf. Barely 30 years ago, Duboeuf was just a wine broker. He was one of the first to offer contract bottling on the spot, travelling around Beaujolais from grower to grower. Today he is one of the biggest merchants in France, but, despite the size of his business, the quality of the wines is still second to none – Duboeuf's reputation is for a particularly pure, light, fruit-driven Beaujolais. For an interesting wine experience visit his Hameau du Vin in Romanèche-Thorins.

Leave Romanèche and return toward the hills in the direction of Fleurie, the next Cru village. Fleurie is a delightful name and a delightful wine, deservedly popular. The local co-operative, the Cave des Producteurs de Fleurie, is particularly good. Up in the vineyards above the village is the little chapel of la Madone. Lunch at the very good Auberge du Cep.

The next village is Chiroubles. Further up in the hills, the wine is consequently lighter and the most delicate of all the Beaujolais Crus. There are two tasting centres, one in the local co-operative, la Maison des Vignerons, the other la Terrasse de Chiroubles further up the hillside, with a wonderful view. You can eat here too. The best of the local producers are Émile Cheysson, Méziat Père et Fils at the Domaine de la Combe aux Loups and Alain Passot.

From Chiroubles drive south to Villié-Morgon which is part of the Morgon Cru. The mountain in front of you, due south of the village on the right-hand side of the road, is the Mont de Py, an extinct volcano. The tasting centre, the Caveau de Morgon, is in the cellars of the Ch. du Parc. The château is unimpressive, but the vast cellars can accommodate as many as 360 people at a time. Recommended growers include Jean Foillard, Jacky Passot, Pierre Savoye and Jean Descombes. Continue around the east side of Mont de Py toward the village of Morgon and follow the signs to Régnié-Durette. Régnié is the newest Beaujolais Cru, created in 1988. Paul Cinquin and Yves Durand are good growers. Near the twin-towered church is the Caveau des Deux Clochers. The Domaine des Hospices de Beaujeu at la Grange-Charton has an impressive vaulted cellar and is worth visiting.

From here it is a short drive to the pretty town of Beaujeu along the D37. There is a tasting centre, the Temple de Bacchus next to the church of St-Nicolas, and you can also buy wine at the Maison de Pays de Beaujeu et Haut-Beaujolais. Allow 45 minutes extra, plus stopping time.

Return to the valley along the D37, and as you approach the road from Régnié the impressive Mont de Brouilly, another extinct volcano, looms up in front. Turn right onto the D43, signposted Odenas, and circle around the hill. The flatter vineyards at its base produce Brouilly and the ones on the hill itself the finer Côte de Brouilly. Many local growers produce both wines, and Beaujolais-Villages as well. To visit the fine 17th-century Ch. de la Chaize and its impressive cellars, drive south on the D43 through Odenas. The wine is good too. Christian Mabeau at Odenas is a good restaurant for lunch.

From Odenas return to the Brouilly hill. A little road on the eastern side (in the direction of St-Lager) leads to the top – how far it is possible to drive depends on the car and the time of year – but the view from the summit is worth a short walk. Continue to the village of St-Lager where the Cuvage des Brouilly (the tasting centre of both Crus) and le Goutillon, a simple place to stop for lunch are located. From St-Lager drive north to Cercié, turn right on the D37 and continue to Belleville, from where it is a short drive back to Mâcon via the *autoroute* or the N6. The Maison du Beaujolais at St-Jean-d'Ardières is a few kilometres to the north. You can taste and buy wine here, as well as eat simple food.

Buying wine is easy in Beaujolais as there are tasting centres in many of the wine villages.

Mâconnais and Beaujolais Fact File

The large, industrial city of Mâcon is the centre of the Mâconnais wine trade but has nothing to compare with the attractions of the surrounding countryside. Belleville is the main wine town in northern Beaujolais.

Information

Office de Tourisme
187 rue Carnot, 71000 Mâcon. Tel 03 85 39 71 37; fax 03 85 39 72 19.

Office de Tourisme
68 rue de la République, 69823 Belleville. Tel 04 74 66 44 67.

Office de Tourisme
Square de Grandham, 69430 Beaujeu. Tel & fax 04 74 69 22 88.

Office de Tourisme
290 rue de Thizy, 69652 Villefranche-sur-Saône. Tel 04 74 68 05 18; fax 04 74 68 44 91. Villefranche is the wine capital of Beaujolais and its tourist office has information on festivals throughout the region, including events surrounding Beaujolais Nouveau day in November.

Maison des Vins de Bourgogne
520 avenue de Lattre-de-Tassigny, 71000 Mâcon. Tel 03 85 38 20 15; fax 03 85 38 82 20. Apply here for all you need to know about wine-tasting and visiting in the Mâconnais. You can eat next door at the Maison Mâconnaise des Vins.

Maison du Beaujolais
69220 St-Jean-d'Ardières, Tel 04 74 66 16 46; fax 04 74 66 30 00 Situated on the N6 just north of Belleville, this wine centre in a typical Beaujolais golden stone building offers facilities for tasting and buying. There is also an unpretentious restaurant serving simple regional food.

Maison de Pays de Beaujeu et Haut-Beaujolais
Place de l'Hôtel de Ville, 69430 Beaujeu. Tel 04 74 69 23 26. Useful wine centre in Beaujolais's traditional capital town. Includes information, lists of growers to visit, exhibition space and wines for sale.

Gîtes de France
Esplanade du Breuil, BP 523, 71010 Mâcon. Tel 03 85 29 55 60; fax 03 85 38 61 98.

Markets

Beaujeu – Wednesday morning
Belleville – Tuesday morning
Fleurie – Saturday
Mâcon – Saturday morning
Villefranche – Monday and Wednesday morning

Where to Buy Wine

Nearly all the main wine villages in both the Mâconnais and Beaujolais possess both a tasting centre, or *caveau*, where you can sample and purchase local growers' wines, and a local co-operative, where you can taste and buy. Quality at the latter obviously depends on the wines on offer. The better co-operatives are listed on pp.68–69. The following list is a selection of local tasting centres.

Caveau du Cru St-Amour
Plâtre-Durand, 71570 St-Amour. Tel 03 85 37 15 98.

Caveau des Deux Clochers
69430 Régnié-Durette. Tel 04 74 04 38 33.

Caveau de Morgon
Château du Parc, Le Bourg, 69910 Villié-Morgon. Tel 04 74 04 20 99.

Caveau de Pouilly-Fuissé
71960 Solutré. Tel 03 85 35 83 83.

Le Cellier de la Vieille Eglise
69840 Juliénas. Tel 04 74 04 41 43.

Château de la Chaize
69460 Odenas. Tel 04 74 03 41 05; fax 04 74 03 52 73.

Fine château with tasting facilities. The cellars are some of the largest in Beaujolais.

Cuvage des Brouilly
69220 St-Lager. Tel 04 74 66 82 19.

Domaine des Hospices de Beaujeu
La Grange-Charton, 69430 Régnié-Durette. Tel 04 74 04 31 05. Dating from 1240, this is now the headquarters of the 82ha Hospices de Beaujeu. The wines are sold by public auction on the second Sunday in October. The building is a national monument and much of the *cuverie* is underground.

Le Hameau du Vin (Maison Duboeuf)
La Gare, 71570 Romanèche-Thorins. Tel 03 85 35 22 22; fax 03 85 35 21 18. George Duboeuf is known as the 'King of Beaujolais' and produces 10 per cent of all the region's wines. His latest venture is this well-presented museum and tasting centre, located in the former railway station, with slides and videos on all aspects of wine-making. There is also a huge sales area selling Duboeuf's wines.

Maison Mâconnaise des Vins
484 avenue de Lattre-de-Tassigny, 71000 Mâcon. Tel 03 85 38 36 70, fax 03 85 38 62 51. Local tasting centre with wine shop and restaurant conveniently situated in the centre of Mâcon. The food is simple but adequate.

Pierre Perrachon
69840 Juliénas. Tel 04 74 04 45 81. Useful shop in Juliénas for wines as well as glasses and corkscrews.

Le Temple de Bacchus
69430 Beaujeu. Tel 04 74 04 81 18.

La Terrasse de Chiroubles
69115 Chiroubles. Tel 04 74 04 22 53.

Festivals and Events

The national French wine fair is held in Mâcon for 10 days every May. Contact the local tourist office for details of events open to the general public.

The Beaujolais region has most of its many wine festivals in the autumn, particularly around Beaujolais Nouveau day; in October there is a Fête des Vins Nouveaux at Jullié. Every village has its Fête du Beaujolais during November and Beaujolais Nouveau is launched on the third Thursday of the month. Fleurie and Brouilly/Côte de Brouilly also have their Concours des Vins.

Other wine events in Beaujolais include Chiroubles' Fête des Crus du Beaujolais in April and, in August, the Fête des Amis de Brouilly in St-Lager.

Where to Stay and Eat

Altéa Bord de Saône Ⓗ Ⓡ
26 rue Coubertin, 71000 Mâcon. Tel 03 85 38 28 06; fax 03 85 39 11 45. Ⓕ Ⓕ
Quiet, modern hotel in the northern part of the town.

Anne de Beaujeu Ⓗ Ⓡ
69430 Beaujeu. Tel 04 74 04 87 58; fax 04 74 69 22 13. Ⓕ Ⓕ
Good restaurant serving hearty local dishes and with a value-for-money lunch menu. There are 7 bedrooms

Auberge du Cep Ⓡ
Place de l'Église, 69820 Fleurie. Tel 04 74 04 10 77; fax 04 74 04 10 28. Ⓕ Ⓕ
Fine cooking but the prices are quite high for the Beaujolais region, where the usual emphasis is on small, value-for-money establishments. Good wine list.

Restaurant du Beaujolais Ⓡ
69460 Blaceret. Tel 04 74 87 54 75. Ⓕ
A good-value bistro just south of Odenas serving regional dishes. Jacques Meyançon and his wife Monique have been here for over 30 years. Try *poulet à la crème* with *crêpes parmentier*.

Bellevue Ⓗ Ⓡ
416 quai Lamartine, 71000

Mâcon. Tel 03 85 21 04 04; fax 03 85 21 04 02. Ⓕ Ⓕ
Central, comfortable and overlooking the Saône river.

The essence of purple-red Beaujolais is its gushing, mouthfilling, thirst-quenching fruit.

Chapon Fin Ⓗ Ⓡ
01140 Thoissey. Tel 04 74 04 04 74; fax 04 74 04 94 51. Ⓕ Ⓕ
Long-established and reasonably priced. Old-fashioned but elegant, with good service and quality cooking. Extensive wine list.

Château de Pizay Ⓗ Ⓡ
Hameau de Pizay, 69220 St-Jean d'Ardières. Tel 04 74 66 51 41; fax 04 74 69 65 63. Ⓕ Ⓕ
Quiet, tastefully converted château set amid its own vines. Most of the luxurious bedrooms are in the annexe. Swimming pool and tennis court. The restaurant features regional dishes and the estate's own wines.

Le Coq au Vin Ⓡ
Place du Marché, 69840 Juliénas. Tel 04 74 04 41 98; fax 04 74 04 41 44. Ⓕ
Good simple cooking at this friendly Beaujolais bistro.

Le Goutillon Ⓡ
Le Bourg, 69220 St-Lager. Tel 04 74 66 82 69. Ⓕ
Simple restaurant on the Brouilly hill, which is often frequented by local growers.

Le Lamartine Ⓡ
259 quai Lamartine, 71000 Mâcon. Tel 03 85 38 97 01. Ⓕ
Simple, good-value bistro situated in the middle of town. Try the menu *grenouilles* (frogs).

Christian Mabeau Ⓡ
69460 Odenas. Tel 04 74 03 41 79; fax 04 74 03 49 40. Ⓕ
Smart tiny restaurant run by a young couple serving good 'modern' food. In summer you can eat on a terrace overlooking the vineyards.

Les Maritonnes Ⓗ Ⓡ
Route de Fleurie, 71570 Romanèche-Thorins. Tel 03 85 35 51 70; fax 03 85 35 58 14. Ⓕ Ⓕ
Comfortable hotel (though a little close to the railway line) with a pretty garden and a swimming pool. Very good but traditional food. Extensive wine list.

La Poularde Ⓡ
Place de la Gare, 71570 Pontanévaux. Tel 03 85 36 72 71. Ⓕ
Old-fashioned décor and the traditional Beaujolais cooking is much appreciated by the locals.

Au Pouilly-Fuissé Ⓡ
71960 Fuissé. Tel & fax 03 85 35 60 68. Ⓕ
Unpretentious bistro with good local cooking.

Le Relais du Mâconnais Ⓗ Ⓡ
La Croix-Blanche, 71960 Berzé-la-Ville. Tel 03 85 36 60 72; fax 03 85 36 65 47. Ⓕ
Friendly, relaxed and comfortable hotel serving hearty regional food. Good wine list.

Daniel Robin Ⓡ
Aux Deschamps, 69840 Chénas. Tel 03 85 36 72 67; fax 03 85 33 83 57. Ⓕ Ⓕ
Here you can eat stylish food on a terrace surrounded by vineyards. A little more pretentious than some of the local restaurants but the service is still friendly. The good wine list contains wines from many local producers.

Rocher de Cancale Ⓡ
393 quai Jean Jaurès, 71000 Mâcon. Tel 03 85 38 07 50; fax 03 85 38 70 47. Ⓕ
Traditional but very competent food in traditional surroundings. Good value.

Wines and Wine Villages

This tour covers two separate wine areas, the Pouilly appellations in southern Mâconnais making mainly white wine, and the Cru villages in northern Beaujolais.

Beaujeu   Once the ancient capital of the region, this small town has an attractive centre. Wine-tastings are held in the beautiful 15th-century Maison des Pays de Beaujeu et Haut-Beaujolais.

Beaujolais AC   Most basic Beaujolais comes from the southern part of the region between Villefranche and Lyon from one of the many local co-operatives. Much of this wine is sold as Nouveau and drunk within weeks of the harvest. Beaujolais Supérieur simply means that the wine has 1 per cent more alcohol – it does not mean a better wine. A tiny amount of Beaujolais Blanc is made from Chardonnay.
Best producers: There are literally hundreds of small growers in the southern Beaujolais, most of whom are members of the local co-operatives or contracted to local merchants. Look for the best merchants, therefore, such as Paul Braudet, Jacques Depagneux, DUBOEUF, Gobet, Loron, Trenel and LOUIS TÊTE. The co-operatives at le Bois d'Oingt, St-Laurent d'Oingt and Liergues have a high reputation. Charmet at le Breuil is one of the few growers who is completely independent.

Beaujolais-Villages AC   This AC is for wine from 39 villages in the north of the region. Fuller and more concentrated, the wine is much better than basic Beaujolais. The best villages are Beaujeu, Lancié, Lantignié, Leynes, Quincié, St-Étienne-des-Ouillières and St-Jean-d'Ardières.
Best producers: Like Beaujolais, this is an AC dominated by merchants and co-operatives. Good independent growers include Ch. de Lacarelle, the largest Beaujolais estate and one of the oldest, at St-Étienne-des-Ouillières, Grands Bruyères and Teppes de Chatenay (both owned by Jean-Pierre Teisseidre), also at St-Étienne-des-Ouillères, Jean-Charles Pivot in Quincié; Dubost at Lantignié and Plateau de Bel-Air at St-Jean-d'Ardières.

Beaujolais Crus   These are 10 villages in the north-east of the region that produce the best Beaujolais. The style of these Cru wines varies considerably – from the lightest wine upward, they are: Brouilly, Côte de Brouilly, Chiroubles, Regnié, Fleurie, Morgon, St-Amour, Juliénas, Chénas and Moulin-à-Vent. The reason for the different styles lies in the underlying geology, but much also depends on the producer. The Crus will be ready for drinking from the summer following the vintage, Moulin-à-Vent needing a further year or 18 months to develop.

In general, these are delightful wines, full of character and crammed with fruit without being the least bit sweet.
Best producers: GEORGES DUBOEUF has a clutch of growers' wines that he makes and sells and other merchants are now increasingly working on the same basis. The Éventail des Vignerons Producteurs is an organization of growers – each one makes his own wine but shares bottling and sales facilities. For other best producers see individual Cru entries in this section.

Brouilly AC, Côte de Brouilly AC   Brouilly is the largest and southernmost Beaujolais Cru with vineyards in several villages around the hill of Brouilly. Côte de Brouilly comes from vineyards on the hill itself. There is a colourful annual wine festival on the summit of the hill in late summer. Brouilly is usually one of the lightest Crus, while Côte de Brouilly is fuller and stronger-tasting since the vineyards on the slopes lap up the hot sun.
Best producers: Ch. de la Chaize, Combillaty (Duboeuf), Pierre Lafond, André Large, Ch. de Nevers (Duboeuf), Ch. Thivin (Claude Geoffray).

Chénas AC   This is a strong, tough Beaujolais Cru, almost in the same mould as Moulin-à-Vent. Most producers of Moulin-a-Vent make Chénas, and vice-versa.
Best producers: Charvet, Duboeuf, Hubert Lapierre.

Chiroubles AC   Up in the hills, this Beaujolais Cru produces light, softly fruity wine for early drinking.

September is a busy time in Beaujolais, when the grapes are picked and brought in from the vineyards.

Best producers: *Émile Cheysson, Javernand (Duboeuf), Meziat (la Combe aux Loups), Alain Passot, Ch. de Raousset (Duboeuf).*

Fleurie AC The third largest and certainly the best known Beaujolais Cru. The name suggests the wine is flowery and certainly it has lots of gentle, velvety fruit. A famous local landmark is the chapel of the Madonna standing guard over the vineyards. The co-operative in the centre of the village, the Producteurs de Fleurie, is well-known.
Best producers: *Michel Chignard, Guy Depardon (Point du Jour/ Duboeuf), Jean-Marc Despres (Clos de la Roilette), André Métrat, Quatre Vents (Duboeuf), Caves des Producteurs de Fleurie.*

Juliénas AC This is one of most underrated Beaujolais Crus. Its reputation is eclipsed by the slightly fuller Moulin-à-Vent and lusher Fleurie wines. The vineyards are on high ground south of the bustling village and the wine develops to a considerable depth.
Best producers: *Clos du Fief (Michel Tête/Duboeuf), Caves des Producteurs de Juliénas, Ch. de Juliénas (Duboeuf), Pierre Perrachon, la Seigneurie (Duboeuf).*

Mâcon AC, Mâcon Supérieur AC Nearly two-thirds of straight Mâcon wine is white from Chardonnay. This should be a clean, youthful, fruity, unoaked wine for everyday drinking. Gamay is used for the red and rosé, though Pinot Noir is also allowed. Mâcon Supérieur has a slightly higher mimimum alcohol level.

Mâcon-Villages AC Most of the Mâconnais' white wines are sold under this AC which is one level up from straight Mâcon. There are 43 villages in the region which can add their own name to that of 'Mâcon-' on the label. Some of the wines can show the nutty, yeasty depth associated with fine Chardonnay.
Best producers: *André Bonhomme, Olivier Merlin, Talmard,* JEAN

THÉVENET *(Bon Gran), plus the co-operatives at Chardonnay, Charnay, Clessé, Igé, Lugny, Mancey, Prissé and Viré. Note also merchants such* as GEORGES DUBOEUF, LOUIS TÊTE *and Trenel. Many of the Pouilly-Fuissé and St-Véran producers make good Mâcon-Villages.*

Morgon AC This Beaujolais Cru comes from vineyards around Villié-Morgon and the hamlet of Morgon. The soil is a little different here and classic

The most recent Beaujolais Cru is Régnié, which, after 9 years of lobbying by local growers, became Beaujolais' tenth cru in 1988. It has not yet made a distinctive mark.

Morgon is easily the most tannic Beaujolais.
Best producers: *Jean Descombes (Duboeuf), Jean Foillard, Jacky Passot, Pierre Savoye.*

Moulin-à-Vent AC This Beaujolais Cru comes from vineyards running down to Romanèche-Thorins and the Saône Valley. There are panoramic views from the famous 17th-century windmill.
Best producers: *Charvet (Duboeuf), Ch. du Moulin-à-Vent (Bloud), Jacky Janodet, Ch. des Jacques, Hubert Lapierre.*

Pouilly-Fuissé AC This AC covers the villages of Vergisson, Solutré, Pouilly, Fuissé and Chaintré (the least good). Differing soils, aspects and wine-making competence mean that the wine does vary. At its best it is a full, rich, opulent

Chardonnay, probably gently oaky, quite high in alcohol but still balanced. The best will last for 5 to 10 years.
Best producers: *Daniel Barraud, Auvigue-Burrier-Revel, Ch. de Beauregard, Georges Burrier, Roger Cordier, Gilles Corsin, J-M Drouin, Roger Duboeuf (sold by Georges Duboeuf), J.A Ferret, Michel Forest,* CH. FUISSÉ, GUFFENS-HEYNEN, *Roger Lassarat, Léger-Plumet, Roger Luquet, Manciat-Poncet, Jean-Paul Pacquet, André Robert, Jacques and Nathalie Saumaize (Saumaize-Michelin), Roger Saumaize.*

Pouilly-Loché AC, Pouilly-Vinzelles AC These 2 small ACs have added the name of Pouilly to their own. The magic name of Pouilly commands higher prices but the wine is often no better than Mâcon-Villages. The Vinzelles co-operative makes 80 per cent of the wine and it could be better.
Best producers: *la Collonge (Gilles Noblet), St-Philibert (Philippe Bérard).*

Régnié AC The newest Beaujolais Cru (1988), which produces a less intense version of Morgon. The village of Régnié-Durette has a distinctive 19th-century church with two towers.
Best producers: *Paul Cinquin, Yves Durand.*

Romanèche-Thorins The vineyards here qualify for the Moulin-à-Vent AC. Duboeuf's headquarters and his Hameau du Vin (see p.66) are in the village.

St-Amour AC This village is the northernmost Beaujolais Cru and produces a firm wine.
Best producers: *Cave Lamartine, André Poitevin (Duboeuf).*

St-Véran AC This AC covers white wine from 8 villages that lie in 2 areas, north and south of Pouilly-Fuissé. Usually unoaked, the wine has more personality than Mâcon-Villages but is less rich than Pouilly-Fuissé.
Best producers: *Gilles Corsin,* CH. FUISSÉ, *Roger Lassarat, Roger Luquet, Prissé co-operative.*

The more open, undulating countryside and warmer climate makes Beaujolais stand apart from the rest of Burgundy, and the region has more than a hint of the South of France about it. As much because of its name as its excellent medium-bodied wine, the village of Fleurie shown here produces one of the most popular wines of the ten Beaujolais Crus. The Gamay vine thrives on the granite soil of northern Beaujolais and the vines are left free-standing, not trained along wires as they are further north in the rest of Burgundy. In the far distance to the left, the Fleurie vineyards give way to those of Moulin-à-Vent, the fullest of all Beaujolais styles.

A-Z of Main Wine Producers

Burgundy is a region of many smallholdings and traditionally the wine was made by the large merchant houses of Beaune and other local towns. The merchants bought grapes from growers who had tiny parcels of land. But these growers are now increasingly making and bottling their own wine, and these are some of the most interesting wines today.

Many growers accept visitors but only by appointment as they don't have time to see everybody who drops by. A letter of introduction from your local wine merchant will help enormously. Some producers don't accept passing tourists at all and even the wine trade has difficulty being allowed in. The local Office de Tourisme or Maison du Vin will be able to help. The following is a selection of the leading producers in the region.

Key to symbols
Visiting arrangements ⊘ Visitors welcome ⊘ By appointment ⊗ No visitors.
Wine styles made ⊕ Red wine ⊕ White wine ⊕ Rosé wine.
Page numbers refer to the tour featuring the producer.

Robert Ampeau et Fils
6 rue du Cromin, 21190 Meursault. Tel 03 80 21 20 35; fax 03 80 21 65 92. ⊘⊕⊕ pp.44, 47, 48
This domaine makes high-quality reds and whites, especially in lesser vintages, from 10ha of vineyards scattered between Beaune and Puligny. The best wines are the Meursault Perrières, Volnay Santenots and Blagny la Pièce sous le Bois. Prices are very reasonable.

Marquis d'Angerville
Volnay, 21190 Meursault. Tel 03 80 21 61 75; fax 03 80 21 65 07. ⊘⊕⊕ pp.44, 49
Back in the 1920s Angerville's father was one of the first Burgundy growers to insist on bottling his own wine. The Volnays are very pure and intense. The Clos des Ducs Premier Cru is in the family's sole ownership. Its other Premiers Crus include Taillepieds and Champans. There is some Meursault too.

Arlot
Route Nationale, Prémeaux, 21700 Nuits-St-Georges. Tel 03 80 61 01 92; fax 03 80 61 04 22. ⊘⊕⊕ pp.22, 33
Since the insurance group AXA took over this estate in 1987 and installed Jean-Pierre de Smet as winemaker it has gone from strength to strength. The reds are light-coloured but intensely flavoured, having been vinified with all the stems. As well as red Nuits-St-Georges, there are Vosne-Romanée Suchots, Romanée-St-Vivant and a rare white Nuits-St-Georges.

Comte Armand
Place de l'Église, 21630 Pommard. Tel 03 80 24 70 50; fax 03 80 22 72 37. ⊘⊕⊕ pp.41, 48
This domaine, under the able management of French-Canadian Pascal Marchand, is the sole owner of the Clos des Epeneaux, the best situated parcel within the larger Epenots Premier Cru. There are now delicious Volnay Fremiets and Auxey-Duresses as well.

Robert Arnoux
3 route Nationale, 21700 Vosne-Romanée. Tel 03 80 61 09 85; fax 03 80 61 36 02. ⊘⊕ pp.25, 33
Son-in-law Pascal Lachaux is in charge at this domaine. Quality is very high and these are lovely concentrated wines which last well. The gems include Échézeaux, Clos de Vougeot, Vosne-Romanée Suchots (probably the best in Burgundy) and Romanée-St-Vivant.

Denis Bachelet
54 route de Beaune, 21220 Gevrey-Chambertin. Tel 03 80 51 89 09. ⊘⊕ pp.31, 32
Denis Bachelet makes minuscule quantities as he has only 3ha of vineyards, but these are carefully made wines and very elegant for Gevreys. Look out for the Gevrey-Chambertin Vieilles Vignes and Charmes-Chambertin.

Ghislaine Barthod
Rue du Lavoir, 21220 Chambolle-Musigny. Tel 03 80 62 80 16; fax 03 80 62 82 42. ⊘⊕ pp.27, 31
This is yet another domaine where a change of generation has seen a sea change in quality. A wine choice of no less than 9 fragrant Premier Cru Chambolles is on offer from one of the region's best female winemakers.

Billaud-Simon
Domaine de Maison Blanche, 1 quai de Reugny, 89800 Chablis. Tel 03 86 42 10 33; fax 03 86 42 48 77. ⊘⊕ p.19
There has been great progress at this 20ha estate in recent years, and its vineyards are superbly situated with 80 per cent on the Serein's right bank, including the Grands Crus le Clos, Vaudésir, les Preuses and Blanchots.

Simon Bize et Fils
12 rue du Chanoine Donin, 21420 Savigny-lès-Beaune. Tel 03 80 21 50 57; fax 03 80 21 58 17. ⊘⊕⊕ pp.38, 49
Savigny's best estate is run by Patrick Bize, one of the best of the new generation of growers. He makes sturdy, harmonious wines with plenty of depth and they are good value too.

André Bonhomme
71260 Viré. Tel 03 85 33 11 86; fax 03 85 33 93 51. ✓❶♀ p.69
This is one of the best-known Mâconnais domaine bottlers. He produces lovely wines from 7.5ha of vines, and delicious honey as well.

Bonneau du Martray
21420 Pernand-Vergelesses. Tel 03 80 21 50 64; fax 03 80 21 57 19. ✓❶♀ pp.40, 48
This 11ha domaine produces only two wines but they come from the best part of the Corton hill. There is a little red Corton, but the main wine is the white Corton-Charlemagne which is frequently Burgundy's finest.

Bouchard Père et fils
15 rue du Château, 21202 Beaune. Tel 03 80 24 80 24; fax 03 80 21 58 17. ✓❶♀ pp.43, 47, 57
This long-established merchant has been taken over recently by the Champagne firm Henriot, which has led to a marked improvement in the quality of the wines. With more than 93ha of vineyards, three-quarters of which are Grands or Premiers Crus, plus others on contract, Bouchard Père has by far the largest Côte de Beaune estate and is now expanding into the Côte de Nuits. Wines from its own vineyards are sold under the Domaines du Château de Beaune label. There is also good Aligoté de Bouzeron.

Alain Burguet
18 rue de l'Église, 21220 Gevrey-Chambertin. Tel 03 80 34 36 35; fax 03 80 58 50 45. ✓❶ p.32

These are sturdy, long-lasting wines from Alain Burguet, a rugged individual who has assembled his 6ha domaine from scratch. His Gevrey-Chambertin Vieilles Vignes is excellent.

Louis Carillon et Fils
Rue Drouhin, 21190 Puligny-Montrachet. Tel 03 80 21 30 34; fax 03 80 21 90 02. ✓❶♀ pp.43, 49
These are beautifully understated wines which last and last. Low yields, elegance and balance from this family-owned domaine are the key. The best wines are the Puligny-Montrachet Premiers Crus les Combettes and Perrières and the Bienvenues-Bâtard-Montrachet of which, sadly, only 2 casks (600 bottles) are made.

Chandon de Briailles
1 rue Soeur Goby, 21420 Savigny-lès-Beaune. Tel 03 80 21 52 31; fax 03 80 21 59 15. ✓❶♀ pp.30, 40, 49
Based in an imposing, early 18th-century mansion, this 13ha domaine produces increasingly good red and white. These include 3 Cortons and Pernand's Île de Vergelesses.

Robert Chevillon
68 rue Félix Tisserand, 21700 Nuits-St-Georges. Tel 03 80 62 34 88; fax 03 80 61 13 31. ✓❶♀ pp.24, 33
Robert Chevillon is one of the best winemakers in Nuits-St-

Georges and his wines, including 9 excellent Premiers Crus, are superb. There is also a rare Nuits-St-Georges white wine.

Château de Chorey-lès-Beaune (Dom. Jacques Germain)
21200 Chorey-lès-Beaune. Tel 03 80 22 06 05; fax 03 80 24 03 93. ✓❶♀ p.47
François Germain and his son Benoît make a very good range of Beaune Premiers Crus (the Teurons and Vignes Franches are superb) as well as good-value Chorey-lès-Beaune and Pernand-Vergelesses village wines. The moated, medieval château offers *chambres d'hôtes*.

Bruno Clair
5 rue du Vieux Collège, 21160 Marsannay-la-Côte. Tel 03 80 52 28 95; fax 03 80 52 18 14. ✓❶♀♀ pp.28, 32
This is a 20ha domaine making very pure, understated wines. The range extends from excellent single-vineyard red Marsannays up to Gevrey-Chambertin Clos St-Jacques and Chambertin Clos de Bèze. There is also a small amount of white and a delicious Marsannay rosé.

Bruno Clavelier
6 route Nationale, 21700 Vosne-Romanée. Tel 03 80 61 12 01; fax 03 80 61 04 25. ✓❶ p.33
This is a new star in the firmament, Clavelier having taken over his grandparents' estate in 1990. He started bottling seriously in 1992. The range includes Vosne-Romanée les Brûlées and les Beaumonts, Nuits-St-Georges aux Cras and Chambolle-Musigny la Combe d'Orveau, all Premiers Crus.

VISITING WINE PRODUCERS

Telephone in advance to ensure that your visit is convenient and that there is someone to receive you. **English-speaking guides** are available at some of the larger merchants and co-operatives. The older generation of growers will be very knowledgeable about their domaine but may only speak French. Some of the younger winemakers now speak good English.

French holidays are often taken in August and so it may not be possible to visit some of the smaller family domaines at this time of year. **Lunchtime in rural France** is still an important occasion so don't arrive between 12 and 2pm. **At harvest time** (September to mid-October) everyone will be even busier than usual and there may be nobody available to help you. **Tastings** will probably consist of samples of the most recently bottled

vintage or vintages and perhaps the latest wines in cask. Do not expect to taste a range of older vintages. **Spittoons** are usually provided at tastings and, whether or not you are driving, it is best to make use of them in order to keep a clean palate. **It is polite to buy** at least a bottle or two, especially if someone has taken a lot of time and trouble to explain his wines. **Credit cards** are not always accepted as payment for wine.

Jean-Francois Coche-Dury
9 rue Charles Giraud, 21190
Meursault. Tel 03 80 21 24 12;
fax 03 80 21 67 65. ⊘❶Ⓨ
pp.44, 48
Low yields, meticulous wine-
making and the judicious use of
new or newish oak have made
these wines some of the most
sought after in Burgundy. Coche
is best known for his whites,
especially Meursault Perrières
and Corton-Charlemagne.

Confuron-Meunier
Prémeaux, 21700 Nuits-St-
Georges. Tel 03 80 62 31 08;
fax 03 80 61 34 21. ⊘❶ p.22
Alain and Sophie Meunier run
this 8ha domaine together. In
recent years, quality has risen
from good to superb. Their best
wines are Romanée-St-Vivant,
Clos de Vougeot and Nuits-St-
Georges les Boudots.

Jacky Confuron-Cotétidot
10 rue de la Fontaine, 21700
Vosne-Romanée. Tel 03 80 61 03
39; fax 03 80 61 17 85. ⊘❶
pp.25, 33
Old vines, low yields, and a
determinedly individual
proprietor at this 9.5ha estate
result in long-lasting, deep-
coloured wines of real
personality and aging ability. As
well as Échézeaux and Clos de
Vougeot, the domaine has
recently expanded into Gevrey,
and makes Lavaux St-Jacques,
Charmes and Mazis-Chambertin.

Gilles Corsin
Les Coreaux, 71960 Fuissé.
Tel 03 85 35 83 69; fax 03 85 35
86 64. ⊘Ⓨ pp.62, 69
The address is in Fuissé but the
cellar is in Pouilly and the tasting
room in Davayé, and worth
hunting out. This long-
established 9ha domaine has
controlled its own wine-making
since the early 1970s. Pouilly-
Fuissé, St-Véran and Mâcon-
Villages wines are made.

Courcel
Place de l'Église, 21630 Pommard.
Tel 03 80 22 10 64; fax 03 80 24
98 73. ⊘❶ pp.41, 48
Yves Tavant is resident manager
at this 8ha estate, one of only a

small number of really top class
ones in the village. His
Pommard les Rugiens is possibly
Burgundy's best example of this
excellent Premier Cru.

René et Vincent Dauvissat
8 rue Émile Zola, 89800
Chablis. Tel 03 86 42 11 58; fax
03 86 42 85 32. ❌Ⓨ pp.15, 19
Cousins of the Raveneaus, and
their only real rivals for the
crown of Chablis. These are
concentrated, gently oak-aged,
long-lasting wines. Look out in
particular for the Clos and
Preuses Grands Crus and La
Forest from the Premier
Cru Montmains.

Jean-Paul Droin
8 boulevard de Ferrières, 89800
Chablis. Tel 03 86 42 16 78;
fax 03 86 42 42 09. ⊘Ⓨ p.19
The four Grands Crus made by
Jean-Paul Droin are fermented
and/or aged in new oak in a
magnificent vaulted cellar. He
makes other Chablis as well,
such as Premiers Crus Vaillons
and Montée de Tonnerre, and
the results are impressive.

Joseph Drouhin
7 Rue d'Enfer, 21201 Beaune.
Tel 03 80 24 68 88; fax 03 80 22
43 14. ⊘❶Ⓨ pp.43, 47
Now partially Japanese owned,
this famous merchant has
substantial vineyard holdings in
Burgundy as well as an estate,
Domaine Drouhin, in Oregon,
USA. Drouhin is known for its
meticulous wine-making,
retaining all Pinot Noir's inbuilt
delicacy, fragrance and elegance.
The 32ha estate in the Côte
d'Or stretches from Clos de Bèze
at Gevrey-Chambertin south to
Bâtard-Montrachet at Puligny
and is especially strong in
Chambolle-Musigny. Look out
also for the Beaune Clos des
Mouches. There is also a 30ha
domaine in Chablis boasting land
in 4 of the 7 Grands Crus.

Georges Duboeuf
La Gare, 71570 Romanèche-
Thorins. Tel 03 85 35 51 13;
fax 03 85 35 56 58. ⊘❶Ⓨ
pp.64, 68, 69
Known with some justification
as the King of Beaujolais,
Georges Duboeuf produces as
much as 10 per cent of all
Beaujolais, frequently under
individual château and domaine
names, and generally to a very
good standard. He also makes
and blends wines from the
Mâconnais, the Rhône Valley
and the South of France. The
Hameau du Vin at Romanèche-
Thorins is worth visiting.

Claude Dugat
Cellier des Dîmes, 1 place de
l'Église, 21220 Gevrey-
Chambertin. Tel 03 80 34 36 18;
fax 03 80 58 50 64. ⊘❶ p.32
Claude Dugat's small estate
produces simple, ravishingly
beautiful Gevreys: rich,
structured and crammed with
fruit. The wines, cellared
beneath a restored tithe-barn at
the top of the village, include
Premier Cru Lavaux St-Jacques
and Grands Crus Charmes- and
Griotte-Chambertin.

Bernard Dugat-Py
2 rue de Planteligone, 21220
Gevrey-Chambertin. Tel 03 80
51 82 46; fax 03 80 34 16 45.
⊘❶ p.32
Cousin to Claude Dugat,
Bernard Dugat-Py, with a
similarly small estate, has only
been bottling his own wine since
1989. The wines, from low-
yielding vines and made with a
loving attention to detail, are
most impressive and include
Premier Cru Lavaut St-Jacques
and Grands Crus Mazis- and
Charmes-Chambertin. The cellar
is a crypt dating from AD 1075.

Dujac
7 rue de la Boussière, 21220
Morey-St-Denis. Tel 03 80 34 32
58; fax 03 80 51 89 76. ⊘❶
pp.27, 33
Owner Jacques Seysses is an
outsider, his father, a Parisian
businessman, as recently as 1967
acquiring 4ha of vineyards, since
built up to 11.5ha. The domaine

includes Clos de la Roche, Clos St-Denis, Bonnes Mares, Échézeaux and Charmes-Chambertin. Seysses fully appreciates the key role of viticulture in the wine-making process and vinifies with all the stems as well as using lots of new oak. The wines are expensive but first rate.

René Engel
Place de la Mairie, 21700 Vosne-Romanée. Tel 03 80 61 10 54; fax 03 80 51 89 76. ⊘⦾
pp.25, 33
Philippe Engel makes splendidly rich, pure, concentrated wines including Clos de Vougeot and both Échézeaux.

André et Frédéric Esmonin
1 rue de Curley, 21220 Gevrey-Chambertin. Tel 03 80 34 37 25; fax 03 80 34 14 24. ⊘⦾ p.32
Much of André Esmonin's wine comes in as part of a share-cropping contract. These are full, tannic, well-coloured wines for aging. He is one of the few growers who makes Ruchottes, Griottes and Mazis-Chambertin, the best Grands Crus after le Chambertin and Chambertin-Clos de Bèze.

Michel Esmonin et Fille
1 rue Neuve, 21220 Gevrey-Chambertin. Tel 03 80 34 36 44; fax 03 80 34 17 31. ⊘⦾ p.32
Michel Esmonin started bottling his own wine in 1987 and in 1989 his daughter Sylvie took over the estate. It is one of 5 domaines making the Premier Cru Clos St-Jacques. Sylvie's is made in a soft style, similar to Bruno Clair's wine, while Jadot and Rousseau, the other main producers of Clos St-Jacques, make bigger wines.

Joseph Faiveley
8 rue du Tribourg, 21700 Nuits-St-Georges. Tel 03 80 61 04 55; fax 03 80 62 33 37. ⊘⦾⦾
pp.22, 24, 33, 40, 54, 57
This Burgundian merchant also makes excellent wines from its own vineyards, more than one-third of which are in the Côte Chalonnaise. This is classy, imaginative, perfectionist wine-

making, the best of which comes from Clos de Bèze, Latricières-and Mazis-Chambertin, Corton and Nuits-St-Georges. François Faiveley prefers to keep a tight eye on quality and only a few basic wines are bought in these days. Some of the Chalonnaise wines are sold under the name Domaine de la Croix-Jacquelet.

J A Ferret
Le Plan, 71960 Pouilly-Fuissé. Tel 03 85 35 61 56; fax 03 85 35 62 74. ⊘⦾ pp.62, 69
Colette Ferret presides over one of Pouilly-Fuissé's best estates, producing richly aromatic wines which reach their peak only after several years of aging.

William Fèvre
14 rue Jules Rathier, 89800 Chablis. Tel 03 86 42 12 51; fax 03 86 42 19 14. ⊘⦾
pp.15, 17, 19
William Fèvre is a leading exponent of the modern tendency to ferment and age Chablis in new oak as well as heading the fight against expanding Chablis' vineyards onto less good, non-Kimmeridgian soil. He is the largest owner of Grand Cru land, with some 15 per cent of the total, and he owns vines in every one except Blanchots. He also acts as a merchant.

Régis Forey
2 rue Derrière le Four, 21700 Vosne-Romanée. Tel 03 80 61 09 68; fax 03 80 61 12 63. ⦻⦾
pp.25, 33
Régis Forey looks after the la Romanée Grand Cru and then passes the wine on to Bouchard Père et Fils. He also has 5ha of his own vines and in recent years the wines have shown increasing concentration and finesse.

Château Fuissé
71960 Fuissé. Tel 03 85 35 61 44; fax 03 85 35 67 34; ⊘⦾
pp.62, 69

For years Jean-Jacques Vincent at Ch. Fuissé has been the leading producer in Pouilly-Fuissé, making rich, ripe, concentrated Chardonnays. The large 40ha estate also makes a little Morgon and Juliénas, using traditional, non-Beaujolais methods so that they are wines for aging.

Jean-Noël Gagnard
21190 Chassagne-Montrachet. Tel 03 80 21 31 68; fax 03 80 21 33 07. ⊘⦾⦾ pp.42, 47
Jean-Noël, brother of Jacques Gagnard, makes top-quality whites, including Bâtard-Montrachet and the Chassagne Premiers Crus en Caillerets, Morgeot and les Chenevottes, and reds (Santenay, Clos de Tavannes, Chassagne Premiers Crus Morgeot and Clos St-Jean).

Jacques Gagnard-Delagrange
26 rue Charles Paquelin, 21190 Chassagne-Montrachet. Tel 03 80 21 31 40; fax 03 80 21 91 59. ⊘⦾⦾ pp.42, 47
Brother of Jean-Noël, Jacques Gagnard presides over a 4ha domaine, most of which has now been passed down to his sons-in law, M M Blain and Fontaine. Combined family efforts are very good, especially the whites, and include a whole range of Chassagne Premiers Crus (en Cailleret is probably the best) as well as Bâtard-Montrachet, Criots-Montrachet and a tiny bit of Montrachet itself. Jacques' own Bâtard-Montrachet is a yardstick.

Vincent Girardin
Rue de Narosse, 21590 Santenay. Tel 03 80 20 64 29; fax 03 80 20 64 88. ⊘⦾⦾ pp.42, 49
The youthful Vincent Girardin, proprietor of a merchant business as well as a 11ha domaine, is one of Santenay's newest super-stars. These are excellent wines, both red and white, at all levels, and they are fairly priced.

Henri Gouges

7 rue du Moulin, 21700 Nuits-
St-Georges. Tel 03 80 61 04 40;
fax 03 80 61 32 84. ⊘❶⚇
pp.24, 33

Henri, grandfather of today's
Christian and Pierre, was one of
the first to start domaine-
bottling, back in the 1920s. Six
Nuits Premiers Crus are made,
including a les St-Georges and a
rare white Nuits-St-Georges.

Jean Grivot

6 rue de la Croix Rameau,
21700 Vosne-Romanée. Tel 03
80 61 05 95; fax 03 80 61 32 99.
⊘❶ pp.25, 33

Étienne Grivot, son of Jean, is
now in charge at this domaine
which makes a splendid range of
no less than 15 red wines. The
stars are Richebourg, Clos de
Vougeot, Échézeaux and several
Premiers Crus in Vosne-Romanée
(les Beaux Monts, les Suchots and
aux Brûlées) and in Nuits-St-
Georges (aux Boudots and les
Pruliers). Since 1987 the must and
grapes have been cooled down to
macerate for a few days before
the fermentation begins and this
results in rich, concentrated
wines which age well.

Robert Groffier

35 route des Grands Crus, 21220
Morey-St-Denis. Tel 03 80 34
31 53; fax 03 80 34 15 48. ⊘❶
pp.27, 33

Although based in Morey,
Robert Groffier has no vineyards
in the village but he is the largest
landowner in les Amoureuses,
the leading Chambolle-Musigny
Premier Cru. He also makes
Bonnes-Mares and Clos de Bèze.
These are very pure, supple
wines with lovely elegant fruit.

Anne et François Gros

11 rue des Communes, 21700
Vosne-Romanée. Tel 03 80 61
07 95; fax 03 80 61 32 21. ⊘❶
pp.25, 33

When Anne Gros took over
from her father in 1988 the
estate started to bottle its own
wine. There is a sure hand here
and the wines – village Vosne
and Chambolle, Clos de
Vougeot and Richebourg – have
intensity and finesse.

Jean et Michel Gros

3 rue des Communes, 21700
Vosne-Romanée. Tel 03 80 61 04
69; fax 03 80 61 22 29. ⊘❶⚇
pp.25, 33

This is a top source of succulent
red wines of real distinction. As
well as owning vines in the
Richebourg and Clos de
Vougeot Grands Crus, the estate
is the sole owner of Clos des
Réas, a Vosne-Romanée
Premier Cru and has substantial
holdings in the Hautes-Côtes.

Guffens-Heynen

En France, 71960 Vergisson.
Tel 03 85 35 82 71; fax 03 85 35
82 72. ⊘⚇ pp.62, 69

Originally from Belgium, Jean-
Marie Guffens and his wife
Germaine Heynen make
concentrated, splendid (and very
expensive) Pouilly-Fuissé as well
as Mâcon wines. In 1991 he set
up a merchant business under
the name of Verget which sells
white wine only, from top
Montrachet downward. It has
been a deserved success.

Les Hospices de Beaune

Avenue de Stade, 21200 Beaune.
Tel 03 80 24 44 44; fax 03 80 24
45 22. ⊘❶⚇ p.36

Over the years since the 15th
century, the Hospices has been
donated prime blocks of vines up
and down the Côte d'Or,
resulting in a 60ha domaine,
mainly in the Côte de Beaune
and for red wines. The wines are
sold by auction (see page 36)
under the name of the donor or
some ecclesiastical reference
rather than under the name of
the vineyard. Under André
Porcheret's wine-making
guidance the quality today is
high, save for excessive over-
oaking. But the Hospices'
responsiblity is only for making
the wine – local merchants take
over after the sale and it is they
who mature and bottle it.

Alain Hudelot-Noëllat

21640 Vougeot. Tel 03 80 62 85
17; fax 03 80 62 83 13. ⊘❶
pp.28, 33

Alain Hudelot's wines include
Richebourg, Romanée-St-
Vivant and Clos de Vougeot.
Usually the quality is quite
superb but the occasional patchy
wine does occur.

Château des Jacques

71570 Romanèche-Thorins.
Tel 03 85 35 51 64; fax 03 85 35
59 15. ⊘❶⚇ pp.64, 69

Taken over by Jadot in 1996,
this huge 50ha estate produces
unusual but very successful
·Moulin-à-Vent as if the wine
was from Pinot Noir not Gamay,
i.e. with long macerations and
for aging. There is also a white
Beaujolais, called Ch. de Loyse.

Louis Jadot

5 rue Samuel Legay, 21203
Beaune. Tel 03 80 22 10 57;
fax 03 80 22 56 03. ⊘❶⚇
pp.40, 42, 47

A leading Burgundian merchant
and also owner of 50ha of
vineyards. Jacques Lardière is a
superb winemaker, not afraid to
stop the white wine malolactic
fermentations if necessary or to
let the temperature of the reds
climb to 35°C. There is a huge
choice of top-quality wines
ranging from Clos de Bèze,
Gevrey-Chambertin Clos
St-Jacques and many other fine
Gevreys through Nuits-St-
Georges, Corton and Corton-
Charlemagne to a whole host of
Beaune Premiers Crus. The
whites, of which the best is the
Chevalier-Montrachet, les
Demoiselles, are equally fine.

Jacky Janodet

Les Garniers, 71570
Romanèche-Thorins. Tel 03 85
35 57 17; fax 03 85 35 21 69.
⊘❶⚇ pp.64, 69

One of Beaujolais' top estates,
Jacky Janodet makes Moulin-à-

Vent, Morgon and Beaujolais-Villages which age well.

Patrick Javillier
7 impasse des Acacias, 21190 Meursault. Tel 03 80 21 27 87; fax 03 80 21 29 39.
pp.44, 48
The estate boasts only a token barrel or so of Premiers Crus, but offers some splendid Meursault village wines as well as good Bourgogne Blanc, especially the Oligocène blend. A small merchant business, called Guyot-Javillier, is run in tandem with the estate.

Jayer-Gilles
Magny-lès-Villers, 21700 Nuits-St-Georges. Tel & fax 03 80 62 91 79. 〇❶⚇ pp.24, 32
Robert Jayer-Gilles and his son, Gilles, are firm believers in new oak with everything, including their Côte de Nuits-Villages and Hautes-Côtes de Nuits. They also make Échézeaux, where the new oak flavours are more easily absorbed, and Nuits-St-Georges.

François Jobard
2 rue de Leignon, 21190 Meursault. Tel 03 80 21 21 26; fax 03 80 21 26 44. 〇❶⚇
pp.44, 48
The wines from this small estate have marvellous concentration and intensity. Look out for the Genevrières, Poruzot and Sous Blagny – all Meursault Premiers Crus – and the red Blagny la Pièce sous le Bois.

Jean-Marc Joblot
4 rue Pasteur, 71640 Givry. Tel 03 85 44 30 77; fax 03 85 44 36 72. 〇❶⚇ pp.55, 57
You could criticize some of Joblot's wines for being too oaky and he certainly loves to use new wood. But the base wines are more concentrated and have more finesse than those of his peers, and can usually support oak. His Givry Clos du Cellier aux Moines is his best wine.

Michel Juillot
10 Grande rue, 71640 Mercurey. Tel 03 85 45 27 27; fax 03 85 45 25 52. 〇❶⚇ pp.54, 57
A large domaine with 32ha of

PRODUIT DE FRANCE
1991
Mercurey
PREMIER CRU
"Les Champs Martins"
APPELLATION MERCUREY 1er CRU CONTRÔLÉE
75 cl
12% vol.
DOMAINE MICHEL JUILLOT
VITICULTEUR À MERCUREY, SAÔNE-ET-LOIRE, FRANCE

vineyards but still one of the Côte Chalonnaise's best. Sophisticated wine-making produces very clean, pure expressions of Pinot Noir. The whites (including some Corton-Charlemagne) are fine too.

Michel Lafarge
Rue de le Combe, 21190 Volnay. Tel 03 80 21 61 61; fax 03 80 21 67 83. 〇❶⚇
pp.44, 49
Michel Lafarge and his son Frédéric make lovely, fragrant Volnays, including a superb Premier Cru Clos des Chênes – even his Bourgogne Rouge is quite delicious. He is also the sole owner of the Clos du Château des Ducs Premier Cru. Meursault and Bourgogne Aligoté are also produced but the Lafarges' strengths are in their red wines.

Comtes Lafon
Clos de la Barre, 21190 Meursault. Tel 03 80 21 22 17; fax 03 80 21 61 64. 〇❶⚇
pp.43, 44, 48
This is the leading Meursault estate and includes 4 Premiers Crus, a large portion of Volnay Santenots and some of Montrachet itself. Dominique Lafon's wine-making is impeccable and he matures the wines for almost 2 years in barrel in deep, cold cellars so that they last and last. Not surprisingly, prices are high.

Louis Latour
18 rue des Tonneliers, 21200 Beaune. Tel 03 80 22 31 20; fax 03 80 22 36 21. 〇❶⚇
pp.40, 46, 47
This merchant is best known for its whites such as Meursault, Blagny, Corton-Charlemagne and Chevalier-Montrachet les Demoiselles. Latour owns 45ha of vineyards, including major parcels on the Corton hill, some

producing the 'Château Corton-Grancey', the nearest thing to a branded Grand Cru. The Mâcon-Lugny is one of Latour's best-selling wines.

Dominique Laurent
2 rue Jacques Duret, 21700 Nuits-St-Georges. Tel 03 80 61 31 62; fax 03 80 62 32 42. ✖❶
Laurent is an ex-pastry chef who became a smallscale merchant and overnight star in 1992. He buys very concentrated wines and racks from new wood into new wood. The result is very oaky wines.

Leflaive
Place des Maronniers, 21190 Puligny-Montrachet. Tel 03 80 21 30 13; fax 03 80 21 39 57. Also Olivier Leflaive Frères, 3 place du Monument, 21190 Puligny-Montrachet. Tel 03 80 21 37 65; fax 03 80 21 33 94. 〇❶⚇ pp.43, 49
Domaine Leflaive is Puligny's best known estate with extensive holdings in some of Burgundy's top white vineyards, including large portions of the Chevalier, Bâtard and Bienvenues Grands Crus, and most of the Premier Cru Clavoillons. Quality went through a disappointing phase in the late 1980s and early 1990s, but at its best can be exemplary.
The family merchant business, Olivier Leflaive Frères, is very reliable and specializes in Côte de Beaune and Côte Chalonnaise wines.

Leroy
Les Genevrières, 21700 Vosne-Romanée. Tel 03 80 21 21 10; fax 03 80 21 63 81. ✖❶⚇
pp.25, 33
This 23ha estate is run by Lalou Bize-Leroy in tandem with her own personal small Domaine d'Auvernay at St-Romain, and also the family merchant business, Maison Leroy, which is based in Auxey-Duresses. She practises biodynamism in the vineyard, along with severe pruning and crop-thinning, and the result is very low yields. The wines are fabulously concentrated and, not surprisingly, sell for very high prices.

Méo-Camuzet

11 rue des Grands Crus, 21190 Vosne-Romanée. Tel & fax 03 80 61 11 05. ⊘⦿⦾ p.33

Jean-Nicolas Méo has quickly established Méo-Camuzet as one of Vosne's finest estates, despite plenty of competition in the village. The range is large and mouth-watering and encompasses Richebourg, Clos de Vougeot, Corton-Rognets and Vosne Premiers Crus, including the rare Cros Parentoux.

Prince de Mérode

Ch. de Serrigny, 21550 Ladoix. Tel 03 80 26 40 80; fax 03 80 26 47 63. ⊘⦿ pp.40, 48

Based in a converted stable opposite a fine, moated château, this 12ha estate is a splendid source of that elusive wine, top-quality Corton.

Hubert de Montille

Rue de Pied de la Vallée, 21190 Volnay. Tel 03 80 21 62 67; fax 03 80 21 67 14. ⊘⦿⦾ pp.44, 49

This small estate belongs to one of Dijon's leading lawyers. De Montille's wines are rarely chaptalized (adding sugar to the must) and they are all the purer and more delicious as a result. The estate may be modest but boasts 3 Volnay and 3 Pommard Premiers Crus as well as white Puligny-Montrachet le Cailleret.

Pierre Morey

9 rue Comte Lafon, 21190 Meursault. Tel 03 80 21 21 03; fax 03 80 21 66 38. ⊘⦿⦾ pp.44, 48

Pierre Morey leads a triple life – he owns 8.5ha of vineyards, a merchant business called Morey Blanc and he is also the cellar manager at Domaine Leflaive. His Meursaults, whether from his own vines or from bought-in grapes, are rich, concentrated and meant for aging.

Albert Morot

Ch. de la Creusotte, 21200 Beaune. Tel 03 80 22 35 39; fax 03 80 22 47 50. ⊘⦿ p.47

This estate was once a merchant, but now sells its own wine, including 6 Beaune Premiers Crus. Old vines, low yields, and a hands-off approach result in high-quality here.

Denis Mortet

22 rue de l'Église, 21220 Gevrey-Chambertin. Tel 03 80 34 10 05; fax 03 80 58 51 32. ⊘⦿ p.32

Denis Mortet is one of Gevrey's rising stars. He now owns 12ha of vines and makes lovely wines including Chambertin, Clos de Vougeot, and the Gevrey Premiers Crus Champeaux and Lavaut St-Jacques.

Mugneret-Gibourg/Dr Georges Mugneret

5 rue des Communes, 21700 Vosne-Romanée. Tel 03 80 61 01 57; fax 03 80 61 33 08. ⊘⦿ p.33

Much of the estate is tended on a share-cropping or an à la tâche basis, which means being paid for the work done rather than for the hours spent. Look out for the Ruchottes-Chambertin, Clos de Vougeot, Chambolle-Musigny les Feusselottes and Nuits-St-Georges les Chaignots.

J Frédéric Mugnier

Ch. de Chambolle-Musigny, 21220 Chambolle-Musigny. Tel 03 80 62 85 39; fax 03 80 62 87 36. ⊘⦿ pp.27, 31

Freddy Mugnier has been running his small family estate of 4ha since 1984 and with success. You will fine true fragrant, perfumed Chambolles here.

Philippe Naddef

30 rue Jean Jaurès, 21160 Couchey. Tel 03 80 51 45 99; fax 03 80 58 83 62. ⊘⦿ p.28

Philippe Naddef runs this small estate with quiet determination and perfectionism. These are fullish, concentrated wines which last well. The Mazis-Chambertin and Gevrey-Chambertin les Cazetiers are particularly fine.

Henri Perrot-Minot

54 rue des Grands Crus, 21220 Morey-St-Denis. Tel 03 80 34 32 51; fax 03 80 34 13 57. ⊘⦿ pp.27, 33

The arrival of son Christophe in 1992 has done wonders. The wine is now of consistently good quality and all bottled at the estate. The wines are well-coloured with lovely elegant fruit. The star is the Chambolle-Musigny la Combe d'Orveau.

Gilbert Picq et Fils

3 route de Chablis, 89800 Chichée. Tel 03 86 42 18 30; fax 03 86 42 17 70. ⊘⦾ pp.17, 19

Didier Picq is one of the best of the younger generation of Chablis growers producing crisp, stylish wines. Sadly, he owns no Grand Cru land.

Pousse d'Or

rue de la Chapelle, 21190 Volnay. Tel 03 80 21 61 33; fax 03 80 21 29 97. ⊘⦿⦾ pp.42, 44, 49

Gérard Potel, assisted by his son Nicolas, is in charge of this progressive, efficient estate which includes sole ownership of several Volnay Premiers Crus. From the château there is a fine view of the Volnay vineyards.

Ramonet

4 place des Noyers, 21190 Chassagne-Montrachet. Tel 03 80 21 30 88; fax 03 80 21 35 65. ⊘⦿⦾ pp.42, 47

Noël Ramonet and his brother Jean-Claude use traditional methods to produce superb, long-lasting wines, including Montrachet, Bâtard and Bienvenues and some splendid Chassagnes Premiers Crus.

Jean-Marie Raveneau

9 rue de Chichée, 89800 Chablis. Tel 03 86 42 17 46; fax 03 86 42 45 55. ⊗⦾ pp.15, 19

Jean-Marie is one of only a few growers who produce Chablis as it should be: steely, austere, with no exaggerated oaky flavours, yet rich and not for drinking until it is 6 or 7 years old. Sadly, he has only 7ha of vines but this does include 3 of the 7 Grands Crus.

Daniel Rion et Fils
Route Nationale, Prémeaux, 21700 Nuits-St-Georges. Tel 03 80 62 31 10; fax 03 80 61 13 41. ⊘⦿⦾ pp.22, 31, 33
Patrice Rion is one of the most open-minded of the younger generation of Burgundian winemakers. There is a wide range and the wines are increasingly stylish – the best are Chambolle-Musigny les Charmes and Vosne-Romanée les Beaux Monts.

Antonin Rodet
71640 Mercurey. Tel 03 85 45 22 22; fax 03 85 45 25 49. ⊘⦿⦾ pp.54, 57
Now run by the Champagne firm, Laurent Perrier, this well-run merchant with imaginative wine-making also owns or controls and sells the wines of 3 large Côte Chalonnaise estates (including Ch. de Rully) plus the Meursault-based Domaine Jacques Prieur.

Romanée-Conti
1 rue Derrière le Four, 21700 Vosne-Romanée. Tel 03 80 61 04 57; fax 03 80 61 05 72 ⦻⦿⦾ pp.25, 33, 43
Burgundy's most famous estate owns 27ha of vines, all Grands Crus, including all of Romanée-Conti and la Tâche, sizeable parts of Richebourg and Romanée-St-Vivant and a small parcel of Montrachet. Traditional methods give superb, long-lasting wines, but at very high prices.

Joseph Roty
Rue du Maréchal de Lattre de Tassigny, 21220 Gevrey-Chambertin. Tel 03 80 34 38 97. ⊘⦿⦾ p.32
A passionate man, Joseph Roty runs a small estate which includes Charmes, Mazis and Griottes-Chambertin and Premiers Crus Clos Prieur and les Fontenys. These are intense, oaky wines.

Emmanuel Rouget
Route de Gilly, 21700 Flagey-Échézeaux. Tel & fax 03 80 62 83 38. ⊘⦿ pp.28, 31
Rouget looks after 6ha of vines, which include Vosne-Romanée les Beaux Monts and Échézeaux. He practises modern techniques such as leaving out the stems, using plenty of new oak and stressing the importance of scrupulous cleanliness and attention to detail while the wine is in cask. The wines are exemplary but not cheap.

Guy Roulot
1 rue Charles Giraud, 21190 Meursault. Tel 03 80 21 21 65; fax 03 80 21 64 36. ⊘⦿⦾ pp.44, 48
Jean-Marc Roulot makes lovely Meursaults which include a splendid range of Deuxièmes Crus, such as Tillets and Tessons.

Georges Roumier
Rue de Vergy, 21220 Chambolle-Musigny. Tel 03 80 62 86 37; fax 03 80 62 85 55. ⊘⦿⦾ pp.27, 31
A domaine of 16ha, which covers some land that Christophe Roumier, currently in charge, farms on his own account. These include a Ruchottes- and Charmes-Chambertin. The domaine's wines range from Musigny and Bonnes-Mares down to village Chambolle. There is a little Corton-Charlemagne.

Armand Rousseau
1 rue de l'Aumônerie, 21220 Gevrey-Chambertin. Tel 03 80 34 30 55; fax 03 80 58 50 25. ⊘⦿ p.32
Gevrey-Chambertin's leading estate has vines in many of the top local Grands and Premiers Crus, including Chambertin, Clos St-Jacques and Clos de la Roche. These are rich, concentrated wines which age well.

Étienne Sauzet
11 rue de Poiseul, 21190 Puligny-Montrachet. Tel 03 80 21 32 10; fax 03 80 21 90 89. ⊘⦾ pp.43, 49
Run by Gérard Boudot, this is both an estate and merchant. The classy wines include Bâtard-Montrachet and Premiers Crus les Combettes and les Perrières.

Christian Serafin
7 place du Château, 21220 Gevrey-Chambertin. Tel 03 80 34 25 40; fax 03 80 58 50 66. ⊘⦿ p.32
This estate has made great strides in recent years. These are concentrated, quite oaky wines which last well. The top wines are Charmes Chambertin and Gevrey-Chambertin les Cazetiers.

Louis Tête
69430 St-Didier-sur-Beaujeu. Tel 04 74 04 82 27; fax 04 74 69 28 61. ⊘⦿⦾ pp.68, 69
This is a reliable Beaujolais merchant who sells a number of single-estate wines. Tête also owns 10ha of vines.

Jean Thévenet
Dom. de Bongran, Quintaine-Clessé, 71260 Clessé. Tel 03 85 36 94 03; fax 03 85 36 99 25. ⊘⦾ p.69
This leading Mâconnais estate makes rich and concentrated but dry wines, and occasional sweet ones from noble-rotted grapes.

Aubert de Villaine
Bouzeron, 71150 Chagny. Tel 03 85 91 20 50; fax 03 85 92 08 06. ⊘⦿⦾ pp.54, 57
Aubert de Villaine, a director of Domaine de la Romanée-Conti, makes 3 Bourgognes – Pinot Noir, Chardonnay and Aligoté – and all are excellent.

Comte Georges de Vogüe
Rue St-Barbe, 21200 Chambolle-Musigny. Tel 03 80 62 86 25; fax 03 80 62 82 38. ⊘⦿⦾ pp.27, 31
Owners of two-thirds of the Musigny Grand Cru, this old Chambolle estate produces some of the finest Burgundy. The range includes Bonnes-Mares, les Amoureuses and a few token barrels of white Musigny.

Picture Credits Michael Busselle 10, 11. All other photographs supplied by Cephas Picture Library. Photographer Mick Rock except Nigel Blythe 22, 37.

Author's Acknowledgments Russell Hone.

Publisher's Acknowledgments Trevor Lawrence (map illustrations), Aziz Khan (grape artworks), Steven Marwood (bottle photography).